Better Homes and Gardens®

NEW Junior COOK BOOK

BETTER HOMES AND GARDENS® BOOKS

Editor: Gerald Knox
Art Director: Ernest Shelton
Associate Art Director: Randall Yontz
Production and Copy Editors: Paul S. Kitzke,
  David Kirchner, David A. Walsh
New Junior Cook Book Editors:
  Flora Szatkowski, Associate Food Editor
  Diane Nelson, Associate Food Editor
Food Editor: Doris Eby
Senior Associate Food Editor: Sharyl Heiken
Senior Food Editors: Sandra Granseth,
  Elizabeth Woolever
Associate Food Editors: Joy L. Taylor,
  Patricia Teberg
Recipe Development Editor: Marion Viall
New Junior Cook Book Designer: Sheryl Veenschoten
Senior Graphic Designer: Harijs Priekulis
Graphic Designers: Faith Berven,
  Linda Ford, Richard Lewis, Neoma Alt West

Better Homes and Gardens
TEST KITCHEN ®

Our seal assures you that every recipe in the New Junior Cook Book is endorsed by the Better Homes and Gardens Test Kitchen. Each recipe is tested for family appeal, practicality, and deliciousness.

In addition, most of the recipes were tested by children in the Better Homes and Gardens Test Kitchen. The youngsters prepared and tasted each recipe for ease of preparation, clarity, and flavor.

Contents

Welcome to the Kitchen

Cooking—and eating what you make—is fun. You can cook meals for your family, fix your own snacks, and make surprises for parties. Learning to cook is easy with this book. With adult help, read through the following cooking helps. When you've learned these rules, you'll be ready to start your cooking adventure.

Getting ready is as easy as counting to three

1 Find an adult who can help you. Always read through the recipe with your adult helper so you can ask questions. Your helper will show you how to use kitchen tools and will help you handle the hot pots and pans.

2 Get dressed for cooking. If you have long hair, pull it back so it won't get into the food.

If you have long sleeves, roll them up so they will stay out of your way.

Always wash your hands with plenty of soap and water before you start to work.

If you like, put on an apron to keep your clothes clean.

3 Take out all the ingredients and equipment you will need. It is important to make sure you have everything you need before you start cooking. Measure the ingredients to be sure you have enough, and put them all in one place.

Be careful while you're cooking

1 Always use hot pads to handle anything hot. Remember that anything you take out of the oven or off the stove is probably hot and will stay hot for a while. If you've had a metal spoon in a hot dish, it's probably hot, too.

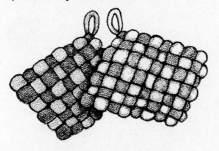

When you bake food, you often have a choice of baking times, because different ovens cook at different speeds. With adult help, carefully open the oven door when the shorter time is up. (The air in the oven can burn you if you work too fast.) Check to see if the food is done, then close the door.

Turn handles toward the middle of the stove so you don't bump them.

2 Spilled food can make you slip and fall. Keep a damp cloth or paper towels nearby to wipe up anything you spill as soon as you spill it. It will make cleanup faster, too.

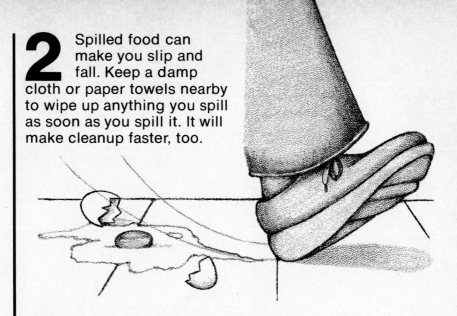

3 Sharp knives are dangerous. Always hold food firmly on a cutting board, and keep your fingers out of the way when you use a sharp knife. Never

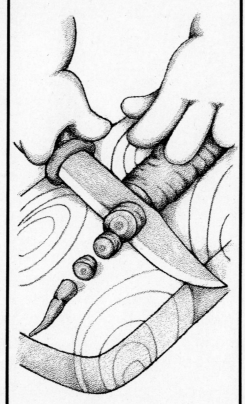

hold food in your hands when you cut it. Be sure your adult helper helps you every time you use a sharp knife.

Be sure an adult is standing by when you use electric appliances—can openers, blenders, and mixers. They can be tricky to use.

There's just one more thing to remember—clean up!

Put away all the ingredients and equipment you have used. Store leftover food. Wash, dry, and put away dishes. Clean up all spills. If you don't clean the kitchen, the head cook may not let you use it again.

Food Guide

Food does lots more for you than just taste good. It helps you grow, look your best, and stay healthy. No one food can do all that, so you should eat many different kinds of food each day.

Eating right isn't as confusing as it sounds. There are four basic food groups you should remember—meat, bread and cereal, milk, and vegetables and fruits. To take good care of yourself, you should eat a certain amount of food from each of these groups every day.

meat

The meat group gives you the protein, iron, and vitamins you need to grow and to build muscles. It helps your blood do its work and keeps you feeling good.

At least twice a day, eat a food from this group. Some foods are beef, pork, lamb, veal, chicken, turkey, fish, and seafood. Also in this group are eggs, cheese, peanut butter, and dried beans.

bread & cereal

Breads and cereals provide carbohydrates, fiber, vitamins, and iron. They give you energy and keep you from being tired. They also help your body use the other foods you eat.

Eat a piece of bread, a bowl of cereal, or ½ cup cooked noodles, rice, macaroni, or spaghetti four times a day.

milk

Foods in the milk group supply calcium, vitamins, and protein. They build teeth and bones, help you grow, and improve your eyes and skin.

Eat (or drink) a food from this group or a glass of milk three times a day. These include milk, yogurt, cheese, ice cream, and other foods made with milk, such as milk shakes, pudding, and custard.

vegetable & fruit

This group has vitamins and minerals for your skin and eyes. And it helps you get well when you are sick.

Four times a day, eat a serving of vegetables, fruit, or juice. One should be high in vitamin C—oranges, strawberries, cantaloupe, or broccoli. One should be high in vitamin A—carrots, sweet potatoes, spinach, squash, or apricots.

other

Other foods not in the four basic groups are eaten mostly for flavor and calories. Such foods as sugar, jelly, soda pop, cookies, candy, desserts, butter, and seasonings make up this group. When you are trying to gain weight, these foods are important, but otherwise, try to eat only a few of them.

Your body also needs water. It is a basic part of blood and other important body fluids.

Chicken Dinner

Cornflake Chicken
Honey-Glazed Carrots
Peanutty Apple-
   Banana Salad
Milk
Yellow Cake

See index for recipes

Your home-cooked chicken tastes even better than the store-bought kind. When you serve it with carrots, salad, and milk, it makes a great-tasting meal that's good for you. Other good choices for a main dish would be Pork Chops in Rice or Frosted Meat Loaf.

Early in the day
Read through the recipes and make sure you have all the ingredients and equipment. Be sure an adult is on hand to help you.
   Make the cake, bake it, and let it cool. Then frost it with Butter Frosting and decorate the cake with colored candies, if you like.

1 hour and 10 minutes before eating
Start fixing the Cornflake Chicken. Brush chicken with the butter mixture and coat it with the cornflake crumbs. Put the chicken into the pan.

50 minutes before eating
Put chicken into the oven. While the chicken is cooking, set the table. You'll need a plate, glass, fork, knife, and napkin for each person. Keep the salad plates in the kitchen for making the salads.

40 minutes before eating
Start fixing the carrots. Peel and slice them.

30 minutes before eating
Start cooking the carrots. Make the salads.

10 minutes before eating
Take lid off the carrots and finish cooking. Put the salads on the table.

At eating time
Take chicken from the oven and put it on a serving plate. Put carrots in a serving bowl on the table. Pour the milk.
   When everyone has finished, clear the table and serve the cake on clean plates with clean forks.

Pizza Party

Personal Pizzas
Hidden Surprise
  Salad
Berry Punch
Brownies

See index for recipes

Have a party for your friends and make all the food yourself. But you can't enjoy a party if you have to spend all your time working in the kitchen.

So make most of the food the day before, then invite your friends into the kitchen to help make their own pizzas. They will like cooking as much as you do.

This menu makes enough food for five people. If you invite more, ask an adult to help double the recipes for pizzas and salad. There are enough brownies and punch for up to ten people.

The day before the party
Read the recipes to be sure you have all ingredients and equipment. Be sure an adult will be there to help you.

Make the brownies. While they are baking, prepare the salad. Cover salad and chill.

Slice hot dogs, pepperoni, and olives. Cover and chill. Cut brownies and cover.

Make the punch *but* do not add the carbonated beverage and ice. Cover punch and put into the refrigerator.

½ hour before the party
Set the table. You'll need a plate, knife, fork, glass, and napkin for each person.

Take out all the ingredients and equipment you'll need for making pizzas.

When guests arrive
Ask guests to help in the kitchen. Roll out biscuits while they put on toppings.

Put pizzas into the oven. While they bake, put the salad on the table and finish making the punch.

Pour the punch and serve the pizzas.

When everyone has finished eating, clear the table and serve the brownies.

9

Weekend Breakfast

Scrambled Eggs
Muffin Surprises
Applesauce
Hot Cocoa
Strawberries

See index for recipes

Start a busy Saturday with a big breakfast. For four people, you'll need to make two batches of scrambled eggs.

If you don't want to start cooking the day before, serve your favorite fruit juice instead of making applesauce.

The day before
Read all the recipes, and make sure you have all the ingredients and equipment. Be sure an adult will be on hand to help you.

Prepare the applesauce. Pour it into a bowl and cover with plastic wrap. Put into the refrigerator until the next day.

45 minutes before eating
Make the batter for the muffins and put into the pans with the jelly.

30 minutes before eating
Put muffins into oven. Set the table. You'll need a plate, mug, knife, fork, spoon, and napkin for each person. Don't forget to put butter on the table for the muffins.

15 minutes before eating
Prepare the cocoa. Leave the cocoa in the pan with the lid on so it will keep warm.

10 minutes before eating
Ask for help to check the muffins. If they are done, remove them from the oven. Prepare the scrambled eggs.

At eating time
Put muffins on a plate. Put applesauce and a spoon on the table. Ladle the cocoa into mugs and top with marshmallows, if you like. Serve eggs on plates and add a few strawberries to make them look pretty.

Measuring

Learning to measure is the first step in learning to cook, because you have to use the right amount of all the ingredients for a recipe to come out right.

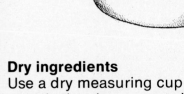

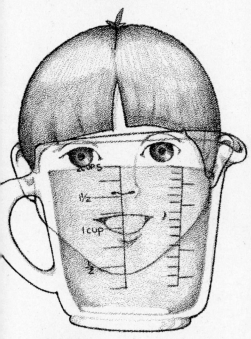

Liquids
Measure liquids (milk, for example) in a glass or clear plastic measuring cup. Put the measuring cup on a level surface, and bend down so your eye is even with the mark. Then pour liquid into the cup until it is up to the mark, as shown.

You will make mistakes if you hold the cup in your hand or read it from above the cup.

Dry ingredients
Use a dry measuring cup exactly the size you need to measure dry ingredients such as sugar. Spoon the ingredient into the measuring cup, then level it off with the flat side of a knife, as shown in the picture above.

Flour
When you measure flour, be sure to stir it well before measuring. This makes it lighter and gives you the correct measurement.

Brown sugar
Pack brown sugar into a dry measuring cup so it holds its shape when the cup is turned upside down. Push it into the cup with your hand.

Butter or margarine
The easiest way to measure butter or margarine is to use one stick (¼ pound) when you need ½ cup, ½ of a stick when you need ¼ cup, and ⅛ of a stick when you need a tablespoon. See picture below.

Shortening
Measure shortening in a dry measuring cup. Pack it with a rubber scraper, as shown, to make sure you are measuring only shortening, not air.

Teaspoons and tablespoons
Use the same set of measuring spoons for both liquid and dry ingredients. These are different from the spoons you use for eating, so be sure to pick the right size spoon.

For liquid ingredients, simply fill the spoon to the top.

Fill the proper spoon, and level off dry ingredients with the flat side of a knife.

11

Words to Know

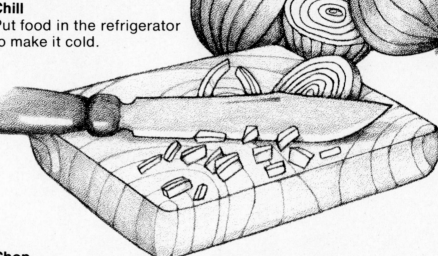

b

Bake
Cook in the oven.

Beat
Use a fork or a wooden spoon in a fast up-and-down motion to mix food. You can also use an eggbeater or an electric mixer. Beating is used to add air to a mixture and to make it smooth.

Blend
Use an electric blender to mix or chop food.

Boil
Cook liquid over high heat so lots of big bubbles form quickly, then break.

Broil
Cook by direct heat under a broiler in an electric or gas range.

c

Casserole
A mixture of foods baked together. The dish used is a casserole dish.

Chill
Put food in the refrigerator to make it cold.

Chop
Cut food into small pieces, using a sharp knife on a cutting board. The pieces don't have to be the same shape, but they should be about the size of peas. You can also chop foods with an electric blender or a food processor.

Combine
Mix foods together.

Constantly
All the time.

Cool
Let food stay on the counter until it is no longer hot. Put food on a cooling rack to help it cool more quickly and evenly.

Cover
Put bowl cover, plastic wrap, waxed paper, or foil over a dish of food to keep air out.

Cream
Beat with a wooden spoon or electric mixer to make mixture smooth and fluffy. Creaming is used in making cookies and cakes to combine the butter and shortening with the sugar. It adds air to the batter.

d

Dissolve
Stir a dry ingredient (like sugar) into a liquid (like water) until it disappears.

Drain
Put food into a sieve or colander to separate the solid part from the liquid.

f

Fold
Carefully mix two or more foods by stirring gently to avoid removing air from the mixture.

g Grate
Rub a food across the smallest holes on a grater to break food into tiny pieces. These are the smallest pieces you can get.

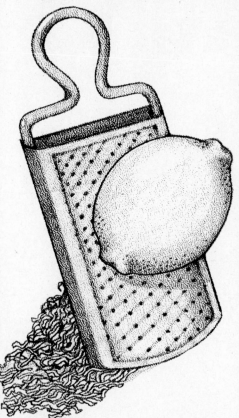

Grease
Rub the inside of a pan with some shortening to keep food from sticking to the pan while baking. Put some shortening on a paper towel, waxed paper, or pastry brush to keep your hands clean. Then spread over the pan. Sometimes the pan is also coated with flour. Look at the picture of a boy greasing muffin pans on page 62.

k Knead
Use your hands to push against dough, then fold it, turn it, and press again to make it smooth.

l Ladle
Dip and serve a liquid or a mixture of ingredients, using a ladle or a measuring cup with a handle.

m Measure
Find the right amount of each ingredient to use in the recipe you're making.

Melt
Turn a solid into a liquid by heating it.

Menu
A list of the foods to be served at a meal. It should include something from each basic food group.

Mix
Stir foods together so the mixture of them looks the same all over.

Main Dish
The main part of the meal. It contains a food from the meat group, such as meat, fish, chicken, cheese, or eggs.

o Occasionally
Once in a while. Usually it means to do something once every few minutes.

p Peel
Remove the outer skin from a vegetable or fruit. Use a vegetable peeler to peel most foods.

s Shred
Rub a food across a shredder to make long, thin pieces.

Sift
Put a dry mixture (like powdered sugar) through a sifter or sieve to break up the lumps.

Simmer
Cook in liquid over low heat so small bubbles form slowly.

Slice
Cut across food to make thin pieces like a slice of bread. See picture, page 49.

t Toss
Mix ingredients lightly in a bowl by lifting them with two spoons or your hands, then dropping them. See picture, page 42.

Equipment

pots & pans

pie plate

skillet

saucepan

baking pan

muffin pan

A skillet or frying pan is more shallow than a saucepan. Baking pans come in different shapes—rectangular, round, and square. Find the right one by measuring it. Ask an adult to help find other pans.

cutting

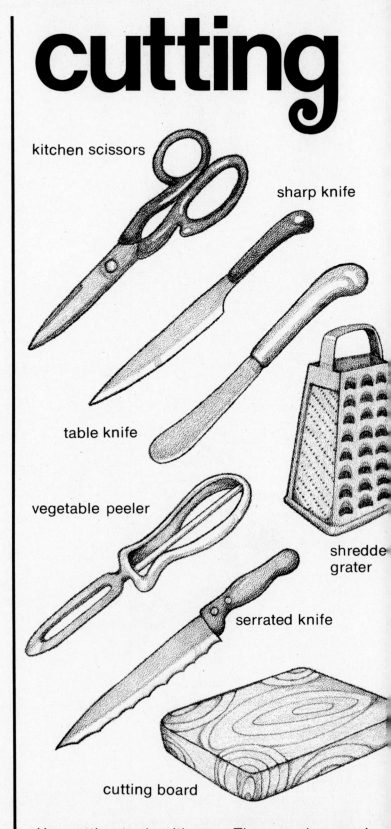

kitchen scissors

sharp knife

table knife

vegetable peeler

shredder grater

serrated knife

cutting board

Use cutting tools with care. They are sharp and can cut you. Notice the different kinds.
Be sure to use the right knife for the job and always cut on a cutting board.

mixing | other things

rubber scraper

slotted spoon

wooden spoon

electric mixer

blender

eggbeater

ladle

pancake turner

colander

sieve

tongs

cooling rack

Electric mixers and blenders should be used only by careful cooks. Be sure an adult helps when you use them. Use a wooden spoon for stirring. It feels good in your hand and won't get hot when you cook with it. Rubber scrapers are good stirrers, too.

Use tongs and ladles for serving foods, colanders and sieves for draining, and a cooling rack for cooling baked goods.

15

Super Sandwiches

Making sandwiches is lots of fun, and it's something you can do even if you have never cooked before. There are plenty of sandwich recipes in this chapter, but you can make up your own, too. Use your imagination. Lots of fruits, vegetables, and meats are good on sandwiches. These two sandwich-makers are putting together Bacon-Tomato Sandwiches (the recipe is on page 23). They are spreading the toast with peanut butter, but you can also use mayonnaise or plain butter.

Taco Burgers

Ingredients

1   pound ground beef
1   8-ounce can tomatoes
1   teaspoon chili powder
1   teaspoon worcestershire
       sauce
1   teaspoon prepared
       mustard
½   teaspoon sugar
¼   teaspoon garlic salt
4   large lettuce leaves
8   hamburger buns, split,
       or 8 taco shells
1   cup shredded American
       or cheddar cheese
    Taco sauce

Equipment

measuring spoons
can opener
10-inch skillet
wooden spoon
paper towels
¼-cup dry measure *or*
   large spoon

1 Break up ground beef into skillet. Put skillet on burner. With adult help, turn burner to medium-high heat. Cook and stir meat with a wooden spoon till there is no pink color. This will take about 10 minutes. Turn off burner.

2 With adult help, drain off the fat. Throw fat away. Be careful because hot fat can burn you. Put skillet back on burner. Add tomatoes and their liquid, chili powder, worcestershire sauce, mustard, sugar, and garlic salt to the skillet. Stir with the wooden spoon to break up tomatoes.

3 With adult help, turn burner to high heat. Cook till mixture boils, stirring a few times.

4 With adult help, turn burner to low heat. Simmer the meat mixture till thick. This will take about 10 minutes. Stir a few times so meat doesn't stick to pan. Turn off burner.

5 While meat is cooking, rinse lettuce with cold water. Pat dry with paper towels. Tear lettuce into bite-size pieces.

6 To serve, put bottom of a bun on a plate. Spoon on some meat mixture, using ¼-cup measure or large spoon. Top meat with some of the lettuce, some of the cheese, and the other half of the bun. (Or spoon meat, lettuce, and cheese into taco shell.) Repeat to make 8 sandwiches. Serve with taco sauce, if you like.

Makes 8 sandwiches.

Hamburgers

Ingredients

1 pound ground beef
Salt
Pepper
4 hamburger buns, split

Equipment

½-cup dry measure
ruler
10-inch skillet
pancake turner

1 Measure ½ cup of the ground beef for each hamburger. This is ¼ pound of meat.

2 Using your hands, shape each part of the meat into a flat, round burger about 3½ to 4 inches across. Put the burgers into the 10-inch skillet.

3 Put skillet on burner. With adult help, turn burner to medium-high heat.

4 Cook burgers till they are brown on the bottom. This will take about 7 minutes. Check to see if they are done by lifting one with the pancake turner and looking at the bottom.

5 Turn each hamburger over with the pancake turner. Sprinkle each burger with some salt and pepper.

6 Cook hamburgers till brown on the bottom. This will take about 4 minutes more. Turn off burner.

7 To serve, lift a burger from the skillet with pancake turner and put it in a split hamburger bun. Repeat with the rest of the burgers. Serve with catsup, mustard, lettuce, onion, tomato slices, and pickle slices, if you like.

Makes 4 sandwiches.

Something Different

Cheeseburgers: You will need 2 slices of American cheese. Cut each slice into 2 triangles. When hamburgers are done on both sides, put a triangle of cheese on each hamburger. Put lid on skillet and let the hamburgers cook 1 minute longer, so the cheese will melt. Turn off burner. Serve as in the recipe above.

Anything Burgers: Make a great-tasting burger by adding an extra filling to your sandwich. Try a creamy salad dressing, taco sauce, cooked bacon strips, cole slaw, sliced olives, or green pepper rings. Or serve the burgers on split onion rolls, rye bread, or toast.

Broiler Burgers: Shape burgers as in the recipe above. Put on rack in a broiler pan. Put under broiler so burgers are about 3 inches from the heat (measure with ruler). Take out of the broiler. With adult help, turn on the broiler. When it is hot, use hot pads to put burgers under broiler.

Cook 6 minutes or till tops are brown. With adult help, remove pan from broiler and turn burgers over with a pancake turner. Put under broiler and cook about 4 minutes longer or till tops are brown. Turn off broiler. With adult help, remove pan from broiler and serve burgers as in the recipe above.

Hot Dogs

Ingredients

1 cup water
4 hot dogs
4 hot dog buns, split
  Butter *or* margarine,
    softened (if you like)

Equipment

liquid measuring cup
2-quart saucepan with lid
tongs
table knife

1 Pour water into the 2-quart saucepan. Put the pan on the burner. With adult help, turn the burner to high heat. Cook till water boils.

2 With adult help, use the tongs to put the hot dogs into boiling water, one at a time. Wait for the water to boil again. When it boils, put lid on pan and turn off the burner.

3 With adult help, move pan off burner. Let the hot dogs stand in the covered pan for 8 to 10 minutes.

4 If you like buttered buns, use the table knife to spread the insides of hot dog buns with butter or margarine.

5 To serve hot dogs, remove lid from pan. With adult help, use the tongs to lift out each hot dog and put on a bun. Serve with catsup, mustard, onions, and pickle relish, if you like.

Makes 4 sandwiches.

Something Different

Curled Hot Dogs: Put a hot dog on cutting board. With adult help, use a sharp knife to make cuts across the hot dog but only halfway through it. Repeat with rest of hot dogs. Cook as in recipe above. Hot dog will curl as it cooks. Serve on hamburger buns.

Hot Dog Octopi: Put a hot dog on a cutting board. With adult help, use a sharp knife to cut hot dog lengthwise from both ends, almost to the center. Roll hot dog onto its side and repeat so that each end is cut into 4 pieces that are still attached. Repeat with the rest of the hot dogs. Cook as in recipe above. Hot dog will look like an octopus. Serve on slices of bread or hamburger bun.

Hot Dog Wrap-Ups

Ingredients

2 tablespoons butter *or*
   margarine, softened
4 slices bread
4 slices American cheese
4 hot dogs

Equipment

table knife
baking sheet
wooden picks
hot pads
pancake turner

Push wooden picks through the bread and cheese and into the hot dog on both sides to hold it in shape while baking.

1 Spread softened butter or margarine on one side of each slice of bread with a table knife. Put buttered side down on a baking sheet.

2 Put a slice of cheese on each bread slice. Put a hot dog diagonally across each slice of cheese.

3 With adult help, turn oven to 375°. It will start to get hot.

4 Fold the 2 opposite corners of the bread over each hot dog. Push 2 wooden picks through the bread and into the hot dog to keep the corners around it, as shown.

5 With adult help, put baking sheet in oven. Bake till bottoms are golden brown. This will take about 10 minutes. Turn off oven. With adult help, remove baking sheet. Use pancake turner to put hot dogs on plates.

Makes 4 sandwiches.

Tuna Salad Sandwiches

You can make these special sandwiches all by yourself, but be sure to talk it over with an adult before you start—

Ingredients

- 1 6½- *or* 7-ounce can tuna
- ⅓ cup mayonnaise
- 2 tablespoons sweet pickle relish
-   Dash salt
- 6 slices white bread
- 6 slices whole wheat bread

Equipment

measuring cup and spoons
can opener
sieve
mixing bowl
fork
table knife

1 Empty tuna into a sieve over the bowl so it drains. Let stand a few minutes. Pour out the liquid in the bowl.

2 Put the drained tuna into the same mixing bowl. Break the tuna into chunks with a fork. Use the fork to stir in the mayonnaise, pickle relish, and salt.

3 Spread about 3 tablespoons of the tuna mixture on each slice of white bread. Top each with a slice of whole wheat bread.

4 To serve, use a table knife to cut each sandwich into 4 squares or triangles.

Makes 6 sandwiches.

Something Different

Egg Salad Sandwiches: Put 6 whole eggs into a 2-quart saucepan. Add cold water to cover eggs. Put pan on burner. With adult help, turn burner to high heat. When water boils, turn burner to low heat, so water simmers. Put lid on pan and simmer for 15 to 20 minutes. Turn off burner. Remove eggs from pan with a slotted spoon and put into a bowl of cold water.

When eggs are cool, remove the shells and throw them away. Put the eggs into a mixing bowl. Mash the eggs with a potato masher or a fork till they are in small pieces.

Follow the recipe above, *but* use the eggs instead of the tuna and add ¼ teaspoon salt. Makes 8 sandwiches.

Fancy Sandwiches: Prepare the tuna mixture as described above. Use a large cookie cutter to cut out shapes from the bread. Spread half the shapes with the tuna mixture. Put the rest of the bread shapes on the tuna to make sandwiches. You can use egg salad to make these, too.

Hot Tuna Sandwiches: Spread the tuna mixture on 4 to 6 hot dog or hamburger buns. Wrap each bun in foil and put on a baking sheet. Put in oven. With adult help, turn oven to 350°. Bake sandwiches for 15 to 20 minutes or till they are hot. Turn off oven. With adult help, use hot pads to remove sandwiches from oven and unwrap them.

Shown on page 16–

Bacon-Tomato Sandwiches

Ingredients

1 tomato
4 slices bacon
4 slices bread
  Peanut butter, butter, *or*
    mayonnaise

Equipment

cutting board
serrated knife
10-inch skillet
tongs
paper towels
toaster
table knife

Slice the tomato with a serrated knife because it cuts through the skin easily. Cut it into 4 or 6 thin pieces.

1 Wash tomato. Put on a cutting board. With adult help, use a serrated knife to slice the tomato, as shown.

2 Put bacon slices side-by-side in skillet. Put skillet on burner. With adult help, turn burner to low heat. Cook bacon till crisp, turning often with tongs. This will take about 6 minutes. Turn off burner.

3 Remove bacon from pan with tongs and put on paper towels to drain.

4 With adult help, toast the bread. Use table knife to spread one side of each piece of toast with peanut butter, butter, or mayonnaise. Put 2 slices of bacon on one piece of toast. Put the other 2 slices of bacon on another piece of toast. Top bacon with tomato slices and rest of toast, plain side up. With adult help, use serrated knife to cut sandwiches in half.

Makes 2 sandwiches.

Something Different

Bacon-Cheese Sandwiches: Make the sandwiches, following instructions at left. Top the tomato slices with a slice of American cheese.

BLT (Bacon-Lettuce-Tomato) Sandwiches: Make the sandwiches, following instructions at left. Top tomato slices with a lettuce leaf.

Bacon and Egg Sandwiches: Make the sandwiches, following instructions at left. Top the tomato slices with a sliced hard-cooked egg.

California Sandwiches: Make the sandwiches, following instructions at left. Top the tomato slices with some avocado slices and bean sprouts.

Peanut Butter-Banana Sandwiches

Ingredients

4   slices raisin bread
    Peanut butter
1   banana

Equipment

toaster
table knife
cutting board
sharp knife

1 With adult help, toast the bread. Use the table knife to spread one side of 2 slices with some peanut butter.

2 Peel banana. Put it on the cutting board. Use the table knife to cut banana in half crosswise and again lengthwise to make 4 pieces.

3 Put 2 pieces of banana on one slice of the peanut butter toast. Top with a plain slice of toast. Repeat with remaining banana and toast. With adult help, use a sharp knife to cut each sandwich in half.

Makes 2 sandwiches.

Something Different

Peanut butter is terrific with many other things on a sandwich. Try something new with this old favorite. Instead of banana, put apple or peach slices on your sandwich. Spread the peanut butter with your favorite jelly or jam, or try honey or marshmallow creme. Or sprinkle it with raisins or shredded coconut. Another time, make your sandwich on white, whole wheat, or cinnamon bread.

Pocket Sandwiches

Make these sandwiches by yourself, but talk to an adult first. Buy the special pita bread in the refrigerated section of big supermarkets or delicatessens—

Ingredients

½ cup mayonnaise
2 tablespoons prepared mustard
2 3-ounce packages thinly sliced corned beef *or* dried beef

2 pita bread rounds
Sliced sweet *or* dill pickles
Shredded Swiss cheese
Lettuce leaves

Equipment

measuring cups and spoons
mixing bowl
spoon
kitchen scissors

1 In mixing bowl stir together mayonnaise and mustard with a spoon.

2 Use kitchen scissors to cut beef into thin strips. Add beef to mayonnaise in bowl. Stir till all meat is coated with mayonnaise mixture. Use kitchen scissors to cut each piece of pita bread in half.

3 Open the bread to make a pocket. Spoon about ½ cup of the meat mixture into each half of bread. Add pickle slices, shredded cheese, and lettuce to the pocket.

Makes 4 sandwiches.

Grilled Cheese Sandwich

Use your favorite cheese: American, Swiss, cheddar, and colby are great—

Ingredients

1 tablespoon butter *or* margarine, softened
2 slices bread
1 slice cheese

Equipment

table knife
6-inch skillet
pancake turner
sharp knife

Hold the skillet firmly while you quickly but carefully turn the sandwich over with a pancake turner.

1 With a table knife, spread butter or margarine on one side of each bread slice. Put one slice, butter side down, into the skillet. Put slice of cheese on top. Put second slice of bread, butter side up, on the cheese.

2 Put skillet on burner. With adult help, turn burner to medium-low heat. Cook till bottom side is toasted and golden. This will take about 8 minutes. Check to see if the sandwich is done by lifting it with the pancake turner and looking at the bottom.

3 Use pancake turner to turn sandwich over carefully, as shown. Cook other side till toasted and golden. This will take about 2 minutes. Turn off burner. Lift out sandwich with pancake turner. With adult help, use a sharp knife to cut sandwich in half.

Makes 1 sandwich.

Something Different

Invent your own sandwich by using a different kind of bread or adding a filling to the cheese. Try raisin bread, rye bread, or whole wheat bread.

Fruit tastes great in a grilled cheese sandwich. Thin apple slices, pineapple slices, or pear slices are especially good.

Add a slice of ham, salami, cooked bacon, or sliced luncheon meat to the sandwich before cooking.

If you like Mexican food, add a rinsed and seeded canned green chili pepper to the sandwich.

Ham & Cheese Toast

Ingredients

½ cup applesauce
¼ cup orange marmalade
    or currant jelly
2 slices Swiss cheese
4 slices French bread *or* 2
    English muffins, split
2 tablespoons butter *or*
    margarine, softened
4 slices chopped ham *or*
    other luncheon meat

Equipment

measuring cups and spoons
small bowl
spoon
table knife
baking sheet
ruler
hot pads
pancake turner

1 In small bowl mix the applesauce and marmalade or jelly with a spoon. Cut the cheese slices in half with a table knife.

2 Put French bread slices or English muffin halves, cut side up, on baking sheet. Use the table knife to spread the bread with butter or margarine.

3 Put baking sheet under broiler so tops are about 4 inches from the broiler (measure with ruler). With adult help, turn on the broiler. Broil till bread is golden on top. This will take 2 or 3 minutes. With adult help, remove pan from broiler.

4 Put a slice of meat on each piece of bread. Spoon about 3 tablespoons applesauce mixture on each ham slice. Put a half slice of cheese on each sandwich.

5 With adult help, use hot pads to put baking sheet under broiler. Broil till cheese melts. This will take 2 to 3 minutes. Turn off broiler.

6 With adult help, remove baking sheet. Use a pancake turner to lift sandwiches to plates.

Makes 4 sandwiches.

Magnificent Main Dishes

The main dish is the star of the meal. It's the answer you get when you ask, "What's for dinner?" Now that you are the cook, you can make up your own answers. Fix your favorites, like pizza, chili, and spaghetti. Or prepare fancier foods, like Oriental Steaks, Pork Chops in Rice, and Cheese Strata. They are not difficult to make. This young man is showing his adult helper how to tell when the Cornflake Chicken is done (the recipe is on page 39).

Frosted Meat Loaf

Ingredients

1 egg
⅓ cup quick-cooking rolled oats
⅓ cup bottled barbecue sauce
½ teaspoon salt
Dash pepper

1½ pounds ground beef
Packaged instant mashed potatoes (enough for 4 servings)
3 slices American cheese

Equipment

measuring cups and spoons
large mixing bowl
fork
13x9x2-inch baking pan
ruler
hot pads
saucepan
table knife
2 pancake turners

1 In the bowl beat egg with fork till it is mixed. Add oats, barbecue sauce, salt, and pepper. Stir to mix well. Add ground beef. Mix in with your hands.

2 Put meat mixture into the baking pan. Use your hands to shape meat into an 8x4-inch loaf. Put pan in oven. With adult help, turn oven to 350°. Bake for 1 hour and 15 minutes.

3 With adult help, use hot pads to remove pan from oven and drain off fat in pan.

4 With adult help, fix potatoes. Follow directions on package, *but* use only *half* the milk. Use knife to spread potatoes over the top and sides of meat loaf to cover it. With adult help, put meat loaf in oven. Bake 15 minutes. Turn off oven.

5 With adult help, remove pan from oven. Put cheese on top. Use 2 pancake turners to put loaf on a serving plate.

Makes 6 servings.

Chili Con Carne

Ingredients

- 1 small onion
- 1 small green pepper
- 1 pound ground beef
- 1 15½-ounce can kidney beans
- 1 15-ounce can tomato sauce
- 1 teaspoon chili powder
- ¾ teaspoon salt
  Corn chips

Equipment

measuring spoons
can opener
sharp knife
cutting board
3-quart saucepan
wooden spoon
ladle

1 With adult help, use a sharp knife to peel and chop the onion on a cutting board. Wash the green pepper. Remove the seeds and stem and throw them away. Chop the green pepper.

2 With your hands, break up the ground beef into the 3-quart saucepan. Add the chopped onion and green pepper. Put pan on burner. With adult help, turn burner to medium-high heat.

3 Cook meat, onion, and green pepper till meat has no more pink color. Stir meat once in a while with a wooden spoon. Turn off the burner.

4 With adult help, drain off fat from pan and throw it away.

5 Add the kidney beans and their liquid, the tomato sauce, chili powder, and salt to the meat in the pan. Stir with wooden spoon to mix well.

6 With adult help, turn burner to high heat. Cook till mixture boils. Stir once in a while. Turn burner to low heat. Simmer, uncovered, for 10 minutes. Stir meat a few times so it does not stick and burn. Turn off the burner.

7 To serve, ladle the chili into bowls. Put corn chips into a dish to add to each bowl of chili.

Makes 4 or 5 servings.

Oriental Steaks

Ingredients

1 green pepper
1 tomato
1 cup cold water
2 tablespoons soy sauce
1 tablespoon cornstarch
½ teaspoon sugar
½ teaspoon salt
2 tablespoons cooking oil
4 small beef cubed steaks
  Chow mein noodles *or*
    cooked rice

Equipment

measuring cup and
  spoons
cutting board
sharp knife
jar with lid
10-inch skillet
slotted spoon
plate
tongs
wooden spoon

Liquid in pan is thickened and bubbly when there are bubbles across the entire surface of the liquid.

1 Wash green pepper and tomato. With adult help, use a sharp knife to remove stem and seeds from pepper and cut it into thin strips. Cut tomato into pieces.

2 Put water, soy sauce, cornstarch, sugar, and salt into a jar. Screw on lid tightly and shake till smooth.

3 Put oil into skillet. Put skillet on burner. With adult help, turn burner to medium-high heat. Add green pepper. Cook till lightly browned. Remove pepper from pan with slotted spoon and put on plate.

4 Put steaks in pan and cook 1 minute or till brown on one side. Turn with tongs. Cook 1 minute or till brown. Put on plate.

5 Shake mixture in jar again. Pour into the skillet. Cook and stir with wooden spoon till thick and bubbly, as shown.

6 Put meat and green pepper into pan. Add tomato and heat through. Turn off burner. Serve over chow mein noodles or rice.

Makes 4 servings.

Cooking Rice

Put ¾ cup long grain rice into a 2-quart saucepan. Add 1½ cups cold water and ½ teaspoon salt. Stir with a spoon. Put lid on pan and put on burner. With adult help, turn burner to high heat. When rice boils, turn burner to low heat. Cook for 15 minutes (do not take off lid). Turn off burner. Take pan off the burner and let it stand for 10 minutes. Makes 2 to 3 cups of rice.

Saucepan Spaghetti

Ingredients

1 pound bulk pork sausage
  or ground beef
3½ cups water
1 15-ounce can tomato
  sauce
1 tablespoon minced dried
  onion
1 teaspoon salt
1 teaspoon dried oregano,
  crushed

1 teaspoon worcestershire
  sauce
½ teaspoon sugar
½ teaspoon dried basil,
  crushed
¼ teaspoon garlic powder
¼ teaspoon pepper
1 6-ounce package
  spaghetti
1 4-ounce package
  shredded cheddar
  cheese (1 cup)

Equipment

measuring cups and spoons
can opener
3-quart saucepan with lid
wooden spoon
ruler
fork
large spoon

1 Break up meat into a 3-quart saucepan. Put pan on burner. With adult help, turn burner to medium-high heat. Cook and stir meat with a wooden spoon, as shown, till there is no pink color.

2 Turn off burner. With adult help, drain off the fat.

3 Use the wooden spoon to stir water, tomato sauce, onion, salt, oregano, worcestershire sauce, sugar, basil, garlic powder, and pepper into the pan. Put pan on burner. With adult help, turn burner to high heat.

4 When mixture boils, break spaghetti into 2-inch pieces and add them to the sauce in pan. With adult help, turn burner to low heat. Put lid on pan and simmer for 30 minutes. Stir often.

5 When spaghetti is done, turn off burner. To find out if spaghetti is done, remove a piece from the pan with a fork. Rinse it under cold water, then taste it to see if it is tender.

6 With adult help, remove pan from burner. Add the shredded cheese and stir till it melts. Serve immediately with a large spoon.

Makes 4 to 6 servings.

Cook the meat, stirring once in a while, till you can see no pink color. You have to stir to brown the meat evenly, but do not stir too much or the meat will break into tiny pieces.

Chicken Pot Pies

Ingredients

1   16-ounce can mixed vegetables
2   5-ounce cans boned chicken *or* 2 6½- *or* 7-ounce cans tuna
2½ cups milk
1   tablespoon instant chicken bouillon granules
⅓   cup all-purpose flour
1   tablespoon snipped parsley
½   teaspoon ground sage
1   package (6 biscuits) refrigerated biscuits

Equipment

measuring cups and spoons
can opener
colander
2-quart saucepan
jar with lid
wooden spoon
6 individual casserole dishes
shallow baking pan
ladle
kitchen scissors
hot pads

1 Put colander into sink. Empty vegetables and chicken or tuna into colander to drain. With adult help, turn oven to 400°.

2 Pour 2 *cups* of the milk and the bouillon granules into the saucepan. Pour the other ½ cup milk into jar. Add flour to jar. Close lid and shake till there are no lumps. Stir mixture into saucepan with a wooden spoon. Put pan on burner.

3 With adult help, turn burner to medium heat. Cook and stir till mixture boils. This will take 6 to 8 minutes. Cook and stir 2 minutes longer.

4 Stir in vegetables and chicken or tuna, parsley, and sage. Cook and stir till hot. Turn off burner.

5 Put 6 casserole dishes into the baking pan. Ladle about ¾ cup of the hot mixture into each dish. Cut each biscuit into 4 pieces with scissors. Put 4 pieces on each casserole.

6 With adult help, put pan in oven. Bake 12 to 15 minutes. Turn off oven. With adult help, remove pies from oven.

Makes 6 servings.

Peachy Beef Stew

Ingredients

2 tablespoons cooking oil
1 pound beef stew meat
1 8-ounce can tomato
   sauce
1 cup water
1 teaspoon salt
3 carrots

2 potatoes
1 onion
1 zucchini
1 16-ounce can peach
   slices

Equipment

measuring cups and spoons
can opener
10-inch skillet
slotted spoon
3-quart saucepan with lid
wooden spoon
vegetable peeler
cutting board
sharp knife
ladle

1 Pour oil into skillet. Put skillet on burner. With adult help, turn burner to medium heat. Add meat to skillet, so meat is in one layer. Cook till meat is brown on all sides. Stir a few times with slotted spoon to turn meat. This will take about 10 minutes. Turn off burner.

2 In saucepan stir together tomato sauce, water, and salt. With slotted spoon, put meat from skillet into tomato mixture. Stir to mix.

3 With adult help, put pan on burner. Turn burner to high heat. When mixture boils, put lid on pan and turn heat to low. Simmer for 1½ hours. Stir occasionally.

4 While meat is cooking, prepare the vegetables. Use vegetable peeler to peel carrots and potatoes. With adult help, use a sharp knife to cut them into bite-size pieces. Peel and chop onion. Wash the zucchini and cut into ½-inch-thick pieces.

5 After the 1½ hours, take lid off pan and stir in vegetables. Cover and cook 30 minutes. Add peaches and liquid to pan. Stir to mix. Cover and cook 10 minutes. Turn off burner. Ladle into bowls.

Makes 6 servings.

Crunch-Top Tuna

Ingredients

8 cups water
1 tablespoon salt
2 cups medium noodles (4 ounces)
1 11-ounce can condensed cheddar cheese soup
½ cup milk
1 9¼-ounce can tuna
1 8-ounce can peas or diced carrots
2 handfuls potato chips

Equipment

measuring cups and spoons
can opener
3-quart saucepan with lid
colander
2-quart casserole dish
rubber scraper
sieve
bowl
paper towel
plastic bag
rolling pin
hot pads
large spoon

1 Put water and salt into saucepan. Put pan on burner. With adult help, turn burner to high heat. Put lid on pan and cook till water boils. Take off lid and add noodles. Be careful, because steam can burn you.

2 When water boils again, turn burner to medium-low heat with adult help. Cook 5 minutes. Turn off burner. Put a colander into the sink. With adult help, pour noodles into colander. Run cold water over noodles to rinse them.

3 Scrape soup into casserole dish with the rubber scraper. Stir in the milk.

4 Drain tuna in a sieve over a bowl. Put tuna in casserole dish. Drain peas or carrots in same sieve. Add to casserole. Throw away the juices. Stir till well mixed.

5 Add noodles to tuna mixture and mix well. Wipe the edge of casserole with a paper towel to clean it.

6 Put potato chips in a plastic bag. Close bag. Use a rolling pin to crush chips. Sprinkle over casserole.

7 Put casserole in oven. With adult help, turn oven to 350°. Bake 50 minutes. Turn off oven. With adult help, remove casserole from oven. Serve with a large spoon.

Makes 4 servings.

Pork Chops in Rice

Ingredients

1 apple
4 pork chops, cut about ½ inch thick
2 cups hot water
2 tablespoons instant chicken bouillon granules
1 tablespoon minced dried onion
1 cup long grain rice
2 tablespoons brown sugar
¼ teaspoon ground cinnamon

Equipment

measuring cups and spoons
cutting board
sharp knife
9x9x2-inch baking pan
spoon
foil
hot pads
tongs
small bowl
large spoon

1 Wash the apple and put it on cutting board. With adult help, use a sharp knife to remove the core and slice the apple, but do not peel. Throw away the core.

2 With adult help, use a sharp knife to cut off the extra fat on the edges of the pork chops, as shown. Throw away the fat.

3 Pour the hot water into the 9x9x2-inch baking pan. Stir in the bouillon granules and minced onion till bouillon is dissolved. Stir in the rice and apple slices.

4 Put the pork chops on the rice and apples. Cover pan with foil. Press foil to sides of pan. Put pan into oven. With adult help, turn oven to 350°. Bake for 1 hour.

5 With adult help, remove pan from oven and use tongs to take off foil. Be very careful, because steam can burn you when you remove the foil. Most of the liquid should be absorbed.

6 In small bowl mix brown sugar and cinnamon; sprinkle over the pork chops and rice. With adult help, put pan into oven. Do not cover with foil. Bake 10 to 15 minutes longer or till meat is tender. Turn off the oven. With adult help, remove pan from oven.

Use a sharp knife to cut the extra fat off the pork chops so the cooked dish will not be too greasy.

7 To serve, use tongs or spoon to lift pork chops to plates. Spoon out rice.

Makes 4 servings.

Hot Dogs and Macaroni

Ingredients

4 cups water
1 teaspoon salt
2 cups wagon wheel
   macaroni *or* 1 cup
   elbow macaroni
1 16-ounce can whole
   kernel corn
1 small onion
1 stalk celery

1 12-ounce package hot
   dogs
2 tablespoons butter *or*
   margarine
1 10¾-ounce can
   condensed tomato
   soup
1 teaspoon chili powder

Equipment

measuring cups and spoons
can opener
2-quart saucepan with lid
colander
sharp knife
cutting board
10-inch skillet with lid
wooden spoon
large spoon

1 Put water and salt into a 2-quart saucepan. Put pan on burner. With adult help, turn burner to high heat. Put lid on pan. Cook till water boils. Take off the lid and slowly add the macaroni. Be careful, because steam can burn you.

2 When water starts to boil again, turn burner to medium heat with adult help. Cook for 10 minutes. Turn off burner.

3 Put a colander into the sink. With adult help, pour the macaroni into the colander. Be careful of the steam. Run cold water over macaroni to rinse, as shown. Empty the can of corn into the colander with the macaroni to drain.

4 With adult help, use a sharp knife to peel and chop the onion on a cutting board. Wash and chop the celery. Cut the hot dogs into bite-size pieces.

5 Put butter or margarine into skillet. Put skillet on burner. With adult help, turn burner to medium heat. When butter melts, add onion and celery. Cook and stir with wooden spoon for 5 minutes.

6 Stir in hot dogs, tomato soup, and chili powder. Put lid on skillet and cook for 10 minutes. Take off the lid. Stir in macaroni and corn. Put on lid and cook 5 minutes longer. Turn off burner. Serve with a large spoon.

Makes 6 servings.

Run cold water over the macaroni in the colander. Rinsing keeps macaroni from sticking together. Turn off water and let macaroni drain while you finish the recipe.

Cornflake Chicken

Ingredients

2 cups cornflakes
¼ cup butter *or* margarine
½ teaspoon salt
¼ teaspoon pepper
8 chicken drumsticks

Equipment

measuring cup and
  spoons
plastic bag
rolling pin
pie plate
6-inch skillet
spoon
paper towels
waxed paper
pastry brush
13x9x2-inch baking pan
fork
hot pads
tongs

Brush chicken all over with melted butter or margarine. It helps crumbs stick and adds flavor to chicken.

1 Put cornflakes into a plastic bag. Close the bag tightly. Use a rolling pin to crush the cornflakes. Pour the cornflake crumbs into a pie plate.

2 Put butter or margarine into the skillet. Put skillet on burner. With adult help, turn the burner to low heat. When butter or margarine melts, turn off the burner. Move skillet off burner. Stir in salt and pepper till well mixed.

3 Rinse the drumsticks under cold water. Use paper towels to dry them. Put chicken pieces on a piece of waxed paper.

4 Brush chicken with melted butter on all sides, as shown. Roll each piece in cornflake crumbs till coated.

5 Put drumsticks into a baking pan. Be sure pieces don't touch each other. If there is any butter left over, pour it over the chicken. Put baking pan into oven.

6 With adult help, turn oven to 375°. Bake till chicken is done. This will take about 50 minutes. Chicken is done when it is easy to poke with a fork. Turn off the oven.

7 With adult help, use hot pads to remove chicken from the oven. Use tongs to put drumsticks on the serving plate.

Makes 4 servings.

Something Different

Potato Chip Chicken: Follow the recipe above, *but* use potato chips or barbecue-flavored potato chips instead of the cornflakes. Crush enough chips to make 1 cup of crumbs.

Personal Pizzas

Ingredients

Shortening
All-purpose flour
1 package (10 biscuits)
  refrigerated biscuits
1 8-ounce can pizza sauce
1 4-ounce package
  shredded mozzarella
  cheese (1 cup)
Use one or more of the
following toppings:
  Sliced pepperoni
  Sliced hot dogs
  Chopped green pepper
  Pickle relish
  Sliced olives

Equipment

can opener
baking sheets
cutting board
rolling pin
ruler
measuring spoons
hot pads
pancake turner

Something Different

Easy Muffin Pizzas: Follow recipe at left, *but* put sauce, cheese, and toppings on English muffin halves. Bake in 425° oven for 7 minutes.

1 With adult help, turn oven to 425°. Grease 1 or 2 baking sheets with some shortening.

2 Sprinkle cutting board with some flour. Pull biscuits apart. Put 1 biscuit on the floured board. Use rolling pin to roll out biscuit till it is a circle 4 inches across, as shown. Put on baking sheets.

3 Repeat step 2 with the rest of the biscuits. Add more flour to the board if biscuits start to stick.

4 Spoon about 1½ tablespoons of the pizza sauce onto each biscuit. Spread evenly over the biscuits. Sprinkle each with about 1½ tablespoons of the cheese.

5 Let each person put favorite toppings on 1 or 2 pizzas.

6 With adult help, put pizzas in hot oven. Bake till crust is brown. This will take 10 to 15 minutes. Turn off the oven. With adult help, remove pizzas.

7 To serve, use a pancake turner to put hot pizzas on plates.

Makes 10 pizzas.

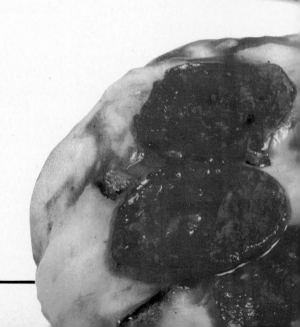

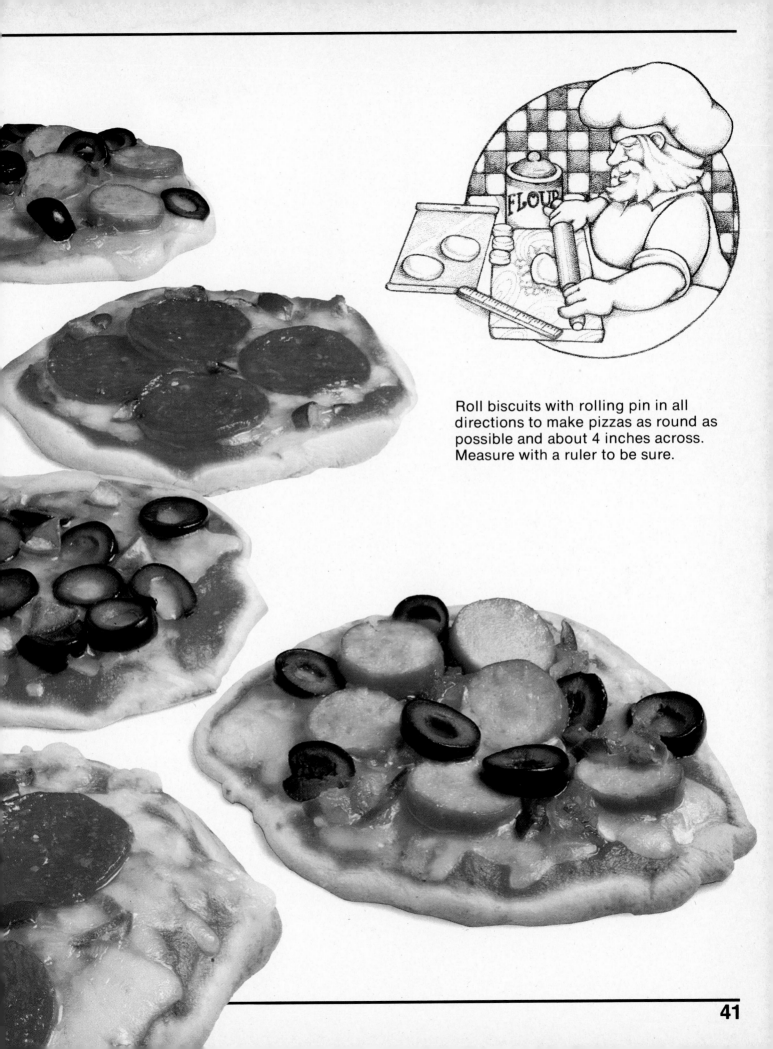

Roll biscuits with rolling pin in all directions to make pizzas as round as possible and about 4 inches across. Measure with a ruler to be sure.

Super Supper Salad

This pretty salad has enough good things in it to make a meal. And you can make it all by yourself after you discuss it with an adult—

Ingredients

1 head lettuce
1 cup cherry tomatoes
1 cup bean sprouts *or* alfalfa sprouts (if you like)
1 3-ounce package thinly sliced fully cooked ham
1 3-ounce package thinly sliced smoked turkey *or* chicken
6 slices American *or* Swiss cheese
   Add 1 or more of these extras, if you like:
   Sliced olives
   Bacon bits
   Sliced hard-cooked eggs
   Croutons
   Bottled salad dressing *or* Shake-Up Salad Dressing (see recipe next page)

Equipment

   measuring cup
   paper towels
   large salad bowl
   salad fork and spoon

1 Rinse lettuce, tomatoes, and bean sprouts or alfalfa sprouts under cold running water. Put on paper towels to drain. Pat lettuce dry with more paper towels. Remove and throw away any green stems on the tomatoes.

2 Tear lettuce into bite-size pieces. Put it into a large salad bowl. Sprinkle tomatoes and bean sprouts or alfalfa sprouts over lettuce.

3 Tear ham, turkey or chicken, and cheese into bite-size pieces. Add to bowl. Add extras, if you like. Toss by picking up and dropping salad, as shown above.

4 Use a salad fork and spoon to serve salad into serving plates or bowls. Let each person pour salad dressing over a salad.

Makes 4 to 6 servings.

Shake-Up Salad Dressing

Ingredients

- 1 5⅓-ounce can evaporated milk
- ½ cup salad oil
- ¼ cup chili sauce
- 3 tablespoons lemon juice *or* vinegar
- 1 teaspoon sugar
- 1 teaspoon prepared mustard
- ½ teaspoon salt
- ¼ teaspoon pepper

1 Measure all ingredients into a *2-cup jar.* Screw the jar's lid on tightly. Shake till ingredients are well mixed.

2 Pour some dressing over lettuce salad or Super Supper Salad (see recipe at left). Refrigerate any leftover dressing and shake again before using.

Makes 1½ cups.

Fish in Foil

Ingredients

- 1 16-ounce package frozen block fish fillets
- 1 small tomato
- 1 small green pepper
- 1 tablespoon lemon juice
- ½ teaspoon onion salt
- Salt
- 2 tablespoons butter *or* margarine

Equipment

measuring spoons
sharp knife
cutting board
foil
shallow baking pan
hot pads

1 Take fish from freezer and let stand 30 minutes. Wash tomato and green pepper. With adult help, use sharp knife to cut up tomato. Remove stem and seeds from pepper and throw away. Cut up pepper.

2 Tear off four 12-inch squares of foil. With adult help, cut block of fish crosswise into 4 pieces. Put a piece of fish on each square of foil. Sprinkle with lemon juice and onion salt. Top with tomato and pepper. Sprinkle with salt.

3 Cut butter into 4 pieces. Put one on each piece of fish. Wrap foil around fish, as shown. Put into pan and then into oven. With adult help, turn oven to 450°. Bake 45 minutes. Turn off oven. With adult help, remove from oven. Unwrap fish.

Makes 4 servings.

Bring foil up and over fish on 2 sides. Roll up other edges.

Cheese Strata

Ingredients

8 slices white *or* whole
   wheat bread
4 slices American cheese
2 tablespoons bacon bits
4 eggs

2 cups milk
1 teaspoon salt
1 teaspoon prepared
   mustard

Equipment

measuring cups and spoons
8x8x2-inch baking dish
mixing bowl
fork
plastic wrap
hot pads

1 Put *4 slices* of the bread next to each other in the baking dish. Put a slice of cheese on each. Sprinkle with bacon bits. Top with remaining bread.

2 In mixing bowl beat the eggs with a fork. Stir in milk, salt, and mustard. Pour over the bread. Cover the baking dish with plastic wrap and leave it out for 1 hour, or keep it in the refrigerator for 1 day.

3 Remove plastic wrap from dish. Put dish in oven. With adult help, turn oven to 325°. Bake 1 hour. Turn off oven. With adult help, take dish out of oven. Let stand 5 minutes. Serve with pancake turner.

Makes 4 servings.

Framed Egg

1 Use a round cookie cutter to cut a hole in the center of a slice of *bread.* Save the center for bread crumbs. Break an *egg* into a small cup.

2 Put about 2 teaspoons *butter or margarine* into a 6-inch skillet. Put skillet on burner. With adult help, turn burner to medium heat. When butter is melted, tilt skillet to coat bottom.

3 Put bread in skillet. Cook about 2 minutes or till bottom is golden. Turn over with pancake turner.

4 Carefully slide egg into hole in bread, as shown. Sprinkle egg with some *salt* and *pepper.* Cover skillet and cook 3 to 5 minutes or till egg is done. Turn off burner. Use pancake turner to lift out egg.

Makes 1 serving.

Break the egg into a cup. Carefully tilt cup and let egg drop into the center of the bread without breaking egg.

Scrambled Eggs

Ingredients

- 2 eggs
- 2 tablespoons milk
- Dash salt
- Dash pepper
- 1 tablespoon butter *or* margarine

Equipment

- measuring spoons
- small mixing bowl
- fork
- 6-inch skillet
- large spoon

1 Break eggs into bowl. Add milk, salt, and pepper. Beat with a fork.

2 Put butter or margarine into a 6-inch skillet. Put skillet on burner. With adult help, turn burner to medium-low heat. When butter bubbles, pour egg mixture into pan. Cook about 1 minute without stirring.

3 Stir eggs with spoon. Cook just till eggs are dry, stirring a few times. Do not stir too much or eggs will be mushy. Turn off burner. Remove pan. Spoon eggs onto plates with large spoon. Season to taste with salt and pepper.

Makes 1 or 2 servings.

Vital Vegetables and Salads

Vegetables and salads don't have to be unloved. In this chapter there are lots of ways to make nutritious fruits and vegetables taste good. The girls in this picture are making a terrific Peanutty Apple-Banana Salad (the recipe is on page 60). The other salads and vegetables you'll find here are just as much fun to make and eat.

Scrumptious Sweet Potatoes

Ingredients

- 2 23-ounce cans sweet potatoes
- ½ teaspoon salt
- 1 8-ounce can peach slices
- 2 tablespoons brown sugar
- 2 tablespoons butter
- 1 cup tiny marshmallows

Equipment

- measuring cup and spoons
- can opener
- colander
- 10x6x2-inch baking dish
- table knife
- sieve
- bowl
- foil
- hot pads

1 Put colander into sink. Empty sweet potatoes into colander to drain. Put sweet potatoes into baking dish. Cut up large pieces. Sprinkle with salt. Empty peaches into sieve over a bowl. Put peaches on sweet potatoes. Save peach liquid.

2 Sprinkle brown sugar over peaches. Pour *2 tablespoons* of the peach liquid over sugar. Save rest of liquid to use another time. Cut butter into pieces. Put on peaches. Cover with foil. Put into oven.

3 With adult help, turn oven to 350°. Bake for 30 minutes. With adult help, remove from oven and remove foil. Top with marshmallows. Put dish into oven. Bake 10 to 12 minutes. Turn off oven. With adult help, remove from oven. Serve with a large spoon.

Makes 6 to 8 servings.

Honey-Glazed Carrots

Ingredients

4 carrots
⅓ cup orange juice
¼ cup water
3 tablespoons butter *or* margarine
1 tablespoon honey
¼ teaspoon salt

Equipment

measuring cups and spoons
vegetable peeler
cutting board
sharp knife
ruler
1½-quart saucepan with lid
wooden spoon
fork
large spoon

Cut carrots into ½-inch-thick slices. Use a ruler to measure the first few slices, then make the rest about the same size.

1 Peel carrots with a vegetable peeler. With adult help, use a sharp knife to cut ends off carrots. Throw away peels and ends. Cut the carrots into ½-inch-thick slices, as shown. Put carrots into saucepan.

2 Use a wooden spoon to stir in the orange juice, water, butter or margarine, honey, and salt. Put lid on saucepan. Put pan on burner.

3 With adult help, turn burner to medium heat. Cook the carrots till they feel tender when poked with a fork. This will take about 20 minutes.

4 With adult help, turn burner to low heat. Take lid off the saucepan. Simmer till most of the liquid disappears. Stir carrots every 2 minutes. This will take about 10 minutes. Turn off burner. Spoon carrots and sauce into serving dish with a large spoon.

Makes 4 servings.

Cooking Fresh Vegetables

Learn how to cook other kinds of vegetables. Ask an adult to help you cut them up and tell if they are done. To cook, put 1 cup water and ½ teaspoon salt in a 2-quart saucepan. Put pan on burner. With adult help, turn burner to high heat. When water boils, fill pan about halfway with the vegetable. Put the lid on the pan and turn burner to medium-low heat. Simmer as long as directions below tell you. Turn off burner. Use a slotted spoon to put vegetables into serving dish.

Broccoli: Trim ends and wash. Cut into long equal pieces. Cook 10 to 15 minutes.
Green Beans: Trim ends and wash. Cut into 1-inch pieces. Cook 20 to 30 minutes.
Cabbage: Wash and cut into wedges. Cook 10 to 12 minutes.
Zucchini: Trim ends and wash. Cut into slices. Cook 5 to 10 minutes.

Two-Way Potatoes

Ingredients

- 4 potatoes
- 2 cups water
- ½ teaspoon salt
  For Buttered Potatoes:
- 2 tablespoons butter
  or margarine
  For Mashed Potatoes:
- ⅓ cup milk
- 2 tablespoons butter
  or margarine
- ½ teaspoon salt

Equipment

- measuring cups and spoons
- vegetable peeler
- cutting board
- sharp knife
- 2-quart saucepan with lid
- slotted spoon
- fork
- large spoon
- *For Mashed Potatoes:*
  - colander
  - potato masher

Peel the raw potatoes with a vegetable peeler. Always peel away from your body so you do not cut yourself.

1 Use vegetable peeler to peel potatoes. Rinse potatoes and put on cutting board. With adult help, use a sharp knife to cut potatoes into quarters.

2 Measure water and ½ teaspoon salt into saucepan. Put pan on burner. With adult help, turn burner to high heat. When water boils, use slotted spoon to add potatoes to the pan.

3 With adult help, turn burner to medium-low heat so water simmers. Put lid on pan. Cook potatoes till tender when poked with a fork. This will take 20 to 25 minutes. Turn off burner. Follow directions at right for Buttered Potatoes or Mashed Potatoes. Serve with large spoon.

Makes 4 servings.

Buttered Potatoes: Use slotted spoon to put cooked potatoes into serving dish. Sprinkle with some salt and pepper. With adult help, pour water out of pan. Put 2 tablespoons butter into pan. Put pan on burner. With adult help, turn burner to low heat. Heat till butter melts. Turn off burner. Pour butter over potatoes.

Mashed Potatoes: Put colander into sink. With adult help, pour potatoes into the colander. Put pan on burner. Measure milk, 2 tablespoons butter, and ½ teaspoon salt into the pan. With adult help, turn burner to low heat. Heat till butter is melted. Turn off burner. Carefully put the hot potatoes into the pan. With potato masher, mash till smooth. Add 1 or 2 tablespoons extra milk and mash in if the potatoes seem too stiff.

Vegetable Soup

Ingredients

1   10½-ounce can
      condensed beef broth
1   soup can water (1¼ cups)
1   16-ounce can tomatoes
1   bay leaf
½   teaspoon salt
½   teaspoon sugar
½   teaspoon dried basil,
      crushed
¼   teaspoon dried thyme,
      crushed

1   potato
1   stalk celery
2   10-ounce packages
      frozen vegetables
      (peas and carrots, lima
      beans, whole kernel
      corn, *or* cut green
      beans)

Equipment

measuring spoons
can opener
3-quart saucepan with lid
kitchen scissors
vegetable peeler
cutting board
sharp knife
wooden spoon
ladle

1 Pour the can of condensed beef broth into the saucepan. Fill the soup can with water and add to saucepan.

2 Add tomatoes with their liquid to the pan. Cut up slightly with the kitchen scissors. Add the bay leaf, salt, sugar, basil, and thyme. Put pan on burner. With adult help, turn burner to medium-low heat.

3 While the tomato mixture heats, ask an adult to help you peel and chop the potato and wash and slice the celery. Add celery and potato to saucepan.

4 Carefully add the frozen vegetables to the soup. With adult help, turn burner to high heat. Bring to boiling. Stir soup with a wooden spoon. With adult help, turn burner to low heat so soup simmers. Put lid on pan.

5 Simmer till all vegetables are cooked. This will take 15 to 20 minutes. Turn off burner. Ladle soup into bowls.

Makes 6 to 8 servings.

Baked Beans

Ingredients

- 4 slices bacon
- 1 onion
- 2 16-ounce cans pork and beans in tomato sauce
- 2 tablespoons brown sugar
- 2 tablespoons catsup
- 1 tablespoon worcestershire sauce
- 1 tablespoon prepared mustard

Equipment

- measuring spoons
- can opener
- 10-inch skillet
- tongs
- paper towels
- sharp knife
- cutting board
- wooden spoon
- 1½-quart casserole dish
- slotted spoon
- hot pads

1 Put bacon side-by-side in skillet. Put skillet on burner. With adult help, turn burner to low heat. Fry bacon till crisp, turning often with tongs so it browns on both sides. This will take about 6 minutes. Turn off burner.

2 Use tongs to put bacon on paper towels. With adult help, pour off the fat. Return 3 tablespoons of fat to skillet.

3 With adult help, use a sharp knife to peel and chop onion. Add chopped onion to fat in skillet. With adult help, turn burner to medium-low heat. Cook till onion is tender, stirring once in a while with a wooden spoon. This will take about 5 minutes. Turn off burner.

4 Pour pork and beans into casserole dish. Stir in brown sugar, catsup, worcestershire sauce, and mustard till well mixed.

5 Use a slotted spoon to lift cooked onions from skillet to bean mixture. Stir in. Put casserole into oven. With adult help, turn oven to 350°. Bake for 1 hour. Turn off oven.

6 With adult help, use hot pads to remove the casserole. Stir beans. Crumble the cooked bacon and sprinkle over beans. Let stand a few minutes before serving.

Makes 6 servings.

Be extra careful when you cook bacon because it can splatter hot fat on you. Turn bacon gently with tongs.

Green Bean Casserole

Ingredients

2   16-ounce cans green
   beans
1   10¾-ounce can
   condensed cream of
   mushroom soup
1   teaspoon lemon juice
½   of a 3-ounce can
   French-fried onions
   (1 cup)

Equipment

measuring spoons
can opener
sieve
bowl *or* measuring cup
1½-quart casserole dish
rubber scraper
paper towel
hot pads
large spoon

Put a sieve into a bowl or cup just large enough to hold it. Empty beans into sieve and let liquid drain into bowl.

1 Put a sieve over a bowl or measuring cup. Empty 1 can of beans into sieve to drain. Put drained beans into casserole dish. Repeat with other can of beans. Throw away liquid.

2 Use a rubber scraper to scrape soup out of can over beans. Add lemon juice. Stir with the rubber scraper till well mixed. Wipe edge of casserole dish with a paper towel to clean it.

3 Put casserole in oven. With adult help, turn oven to 350°. Bake for 30 minutes. Ask an adult to help you use hot pads to remove casserole from oven.

4 Sprinkle the French-fried onions over casserole. With adult help, put casserole back into oven. Bake 5 minutes. Turn off oven. With adult help, remove casserole. Serve with a large spoon.

Makes 6 servings.

Canned and Frozen Vegetables

Canned Vegetables: These vegetables are already cooked, so all you have to do is heat them. Empty vegetable and its liquid into a saucepan. Put pan on burner. With adult help, turn burner to high heat. When mixture boils, turn burner to medium-low heat and cook till vegetable is hot. This will take about 5 minutes. Turn off burner. Lift vegetable from pan with a slotted spoon, and put into serving dish. Top with a little butter, if you like.

Frozen Vegetables: Most frozen vegetables are cooked in boiling salted water. With adult help, follow the directions printed on the package. Don't forget to turn off the burner.

Orange-Applesauce Salad

Ingredients

- 1 3-ounce package orange-flavored gelatin
- Water
- 1 8-ounce can applesauce
- 1 apple
- ½ cup lemon-lime carbonated beverage *or* cold water

Equipment

- measuring cups
- can opener
- mixing bowl
- teakettle
- wooden spoon *or* rubber scraper
- cutting board
- sharp knife
- 4 small bowls

1 Put the orange-flavored gelatin into the mixing bowl.

2 Put 1½ cups of water into the teakettle. Put kettle on burner. With adult help, turn burner to high heat. When water boils, turn off burner. With adult help, measure 1 cup boiling water. Pour the boiling water into the bowl with the gelatin. Stir with wooden spoon or rubber scraper till all gelatin dissolves.

3 Stir in the applesauce till mixed. Put bowl into the refrigerator.

4 Wash the apple and put it on the cutting board. With adult help, use a sharp knife to remove the core. Throw it away. Cut the apple into bite-size pieces.

5 Remove bowl from refrigerator. Stir in the apple pieces and the lemon-lime beverage or cold water. Pour the mixture into 4 small bowls.

6 Put bowls into the refrigerator and chill till firm. This will take about 3 hours.

Makes 4 servings.

Scalloped Corn

Ingredients

- 22 saltine crackers
- 1 egg
- 1 cup milk
- ½ teaspoon minced dried onion
- ¼ teaspoon salt
- Dash pepper
- 1 17-ounce can cream-style corn
- 1 tablespoon butter *or* margarine

Equipment

- measuring cups and spoons
- can opener
- heavy plastic bag
- rolling pin
- 1-quart casserole dish
- fork
- small bowl
- small skillet
- spoon
- table knife
- hot pads

1 Put crackers into plastic bag. Close bag and crush crackers with rolling pin.

2 In casserole dish beat egg with fork. Stir in milk, onion, salt, and pepper. Measure ⅔ cup cracker crumbs and add to milk mixture. Add corn and stir. Put rest of crumbs into small bowl.

3 Put butter or margarine into skillet. Put on burner. With adult help, turn burner to low heat. Heat till butter melts. Turn off burner. Pour over crumbs in bowl. Stir to mix well.

4 Sprinkle crumbs over corn mixture. Put into oven. With adult help, turn oven to 350°. Bake 1 hour or till knife stuck near center comes out clean. Turn off oven. With adult help, use hot pads to remove casserole. If you like, top with green pepper rings.

Makes 6 servings.

Applesauce

Ingredients

4 cooking apples
⅓ cup water
2 inches stick cinnamon
   (if you like)
3 tablespoons sugar

Equipment

measuring cup and
   spoon
vegetable peeler
cutting board
sharp knife
2-quart saucepan with lid
fork
slotted spoon
potato masher
spoon

Mash the cooked apples with a potato masher till the applesauce is as smooth as you like it.

1 Peel apples with vegetable peeler. Put on a cutting board. With adult help, cut apples into quarters and remove the cores. Throw away the cores. Put apples into saucepan. Add water and cinnamon. Put the pan on burner.

2 With adult help, turn burner to high heat. When water boils, turn burner to low. Put lid on pan and simmer till apples feel tender when poked with a fork. This will take 8 to 10 minutes. Turn off burner.

3 With adult help, remove pan from burner. Take lid off pan and remove stick cinnamon with a slotted spoon. Throw it away. Mash apples with potato masher or fork till almost smooth. Stir in the sugar.

4 Spoon applesauce into dishes to serve warm. Or cool, then cover with plastic wrap or foil, and chill.

Makes 4 servings.

Something Different

No-Cook Applesauce: Wash 4 *cooking apples* and peel with vegetable peeler. Put on a cutting board. With adult help, use a sharp knife to core the apples. Throw the cores away. Cut the apples into pieces.

Put apple pieces into blender container. Add ¼ cup *sugar*, ¼ cup *water*, and 1 tablespoon *lemon juice*.

With adult help, cover blender and blend till apples are almost smooth. This will take 30 to 60 seconds. Stop blender and push mixture down with rubber scraper, if needed.

Pour applesauce into serving bowls and sprinkle with a little ground *cinnamon* or ground *nutmeg*, if you like. Serve right away or applesauce will turn brown. Makes 4 servings.

Hidden Surprise Salad

Here's a salad for the family you can make by yourself. Be sure to talk to an adult about it first—

Ingredients

Lettuce leaves
1 17-ounce can fruit cocktail
1 cup cream-style cottage cheese
1 tablespoon honey

Equipment

measuring cups and spoons
can opener
paper towels
1½-quart glass bowl
sieve
2 small bowls

spoon
rubber scraper
plastic wrap *or* foil
large spoon

1 Wash the lettuce under cold running water. Pat dry with paper towels. Tear lettuce into bite-size pieces and measure 2 cups, packing lightly into measuring cup. Put *1 cup* of the lettuce into 1½-quart bowl.

2 Put sieve over small bowl. Empty the can of fruit cocktail into the sieve to drain (save juice to use another time). Spoon fruit cocktail over lettuce in bowl. Put the other cup of the lettuce over the fruit.

3 In small bowl stir together the cottage cheese and honey with rubber scraper. Spoon cottage cheese mixture over lettuce. Use rubber scraper to spread so it covers all the lettuce, as shown. Cover with plastic wrap or foil. Chill several hours or overnight. Serve with a large spoon.

Makes 6 servings.

Something Different

Make your own hidden surprise by changing some of the ingredients in this salad. Instead of fruit cocktail, use cut-up canned peaches, pears, or mandarin orange sections. If you like, you can use orange marmalade or strawberry jam instead of honey.

Spread cottage cheese mixture over the fruit and lettuce so they are hidden. Use a rubber scraper for easy spreading.

Pineapple-Carrot Salad

Ingredients

1 8¼-ounce can pineapple
    slices
2 carrots
¼ cup raisins
¼ cup pineapple *or* orange
    yogurt
   Lettuce leaves

Equipment

measuring cup
can opener
fork
paper towels
cutting board
sharp knife
shredder
mixing bowl
rubber scraper
4 salad plates
ice cream scoop

1 Use a fork to put pineapple on paper towels to drain. Save juice to use another time.

2 Wash carrots. Put on cutting board. With adult help, use a sharp knife to cut ends from the carrots. Shred the carrots. Put into the bowl.

3 Add the raisins and yogurt to carrots. Stir with a rubber scraper till well mixed.

4 For each serving, put lettuce on a salad plate. Put a pineapple slice on the lettuce. Use an ice cream scoop to put some carrot mixture on each pineapple slice.

Makes 4 servings.

Potato Salad

Ingredients

2 eggs
Water
½ teaspoon salt
4 potatoes
2 stalks celery
2 green onions

½ cup mayonnaise
1 tablespoon prepared
  mustard
1 teaspoon salt
¼ teaspoon pepper

Equipment

measuring cups and spoons
2 saucepans with lids
slotted spoon
mixing bowls
cutting board
sharp knife
rubber scraper
fork
table knife

1 Put eggs into small saucepan. Cover with cold water. Put pan on burner. With adult help, turn burner to high heat. When water boils, turn to low heat. Put lid on pan and simmer 15 to 20 minutes. Turn off burner. Use slotted spoon to put eggs into a bowl of cold water.

2 Put 5 cups water and ½ teaspoon salt into 3-quart saucepan. Put pan on burner. With adult help, turn burner to high heat. Heat till boiling. Wash potatoes. Put into boiling water with slotted spoon. Turn burner to low heat and put lid on pan.

3 Simmer 30 to 40 minutes or till tender. Turn off burner. Remove potatoes with slotted spoon. Cool slightly.

4 Wash celery and green onions. With adult help, trim and slice celery and green onions. Put into large bowl. Add mayonnaise, mustard, 1 teaspoon salt, and pepper. Mix well with rubber scraper.

5 Put warm potato on cutting board. Put fork into potato. Pull away the peel with table knife. Still holding it with the fork, cut potato into cubes. Add to bowl. Repeat with rest of potatoes.

6 Peel and cut up eggs. Add to bowl. Carefully mix with rubber scraper. Cover and chill 3 to 4 hours. If you like, put salad into a salad bowl lined with lettuce. Serve with a large spoon.

Makes 4 to 6 servings.

Peanutty Apple-Banana Salad

Ingredients

½ cup mayonnaise
1 tablespoon peanut butter
2 apples
2 bananas
  Lettuce leaves
¼ cup peanuts

Equipment

measuring cups and
  spoons
mixing bowl
rubber scraper
cutting board
sharp knife
table knife
6 salad plates

Cut the apple in half to form a solid base for cutting it. Cut out the core and throw it away. Cut up apple.

1 Measure mayonnaise and peanut butter into mixing bowl. Use a rubber scraper to stir till well mixed.

2 Wash the apples and put on cutting board. With adult help, use a sharp knife to cut the apples into bite-size pieces, as shown. Throw away the cores. Add apple pieces to peanut butter mixture. Stir till apple pieces are coated.

3 Peel a banana and put it on a cutting board. Use a table knife to cut the banana into slices. Repeat with other banana. Add to peanut butter mixture. Stir till all banana slices are coated.

4 Put lettuce leaves on 6 salad plates. Spoon the apple-banana mixture onto lettuce and sprinkle with peanuts.

Makes 6 servings.

Something Different

This salad can be made with many different kinds of fruit. Choose your favorites and use about 2 or 3 cups of the cut-up fruit in place of the apples and bananas.

Try fresh green grapes, fresh orange sections, cut-up fresh or canned pears, canned fruit cocktail, or canned pineapple chunks.

Another time, substitute flaked coconut, raisins, shelled sunflower seeds, or another kind of nuts for the peanuts.

Just-for-Fun Salads

Smiling Bug: Put a canned *peach half* on a *lettuce*-lined plate. Use *raisins* for eyes, *cherry stems* for antennae, and half a *maraschino cherry* slice for the mouth. The legs are made of *carrot curls* (see directions at right).

Carrot Curls: Use a vegetable peeler to peel wide strips from a *carrot*. Roll up each strip and fasten with a wooden pick. Put curls into a bowl of *ice water* for a few minutes to make them crisp. Remove wooden picks before using.

Twin Mice: Put 2 canned *pear halves* on a *lettuce*-lined plate. Put 2 whole *cloves* on each for eyes, 2 *raisins* for noses, and *carrot curls* for tails (see directions at right). For the ears, cut a *marshmallow* into slices with kitchen scissors. Attach to pear halves with wooden picks.

Flower Salad: With adult help, use a sharp knife to cut *tomato* into wedges. Put wedges in a circle on a *lettuce*-lined plate. Top with a spoonful of *cottage cheese* and an *olive* slice.

Best Breads

Baking bread is as much fun as anything, especially on cold or rainy days when you can't go outside. And nothing tastes better than fresh bread, still warm from the oven.

These three young cooks are making No-Knead Yeast Rolls (the recipe is on page 69). They have already made a loaf and more rolls from the same recipe.

The rolls will taste delicious with a meal, while the loaf makes terrific toast or sandwiches. Other breads you can learn to make in this chapter are pancakes, French toast, muffins, biscuits, corn bread, coffee cake, and pumpkin bread.

Muffin Surprises

Ingredients

Shortening
1¾ cups all-purpose flour
¼ cup sugar
2½ teaspoons baking powder
¾ teaspoon salt
1 egg
¾ cup milk
⅓ cup cooking oil
Jelly *or* jam

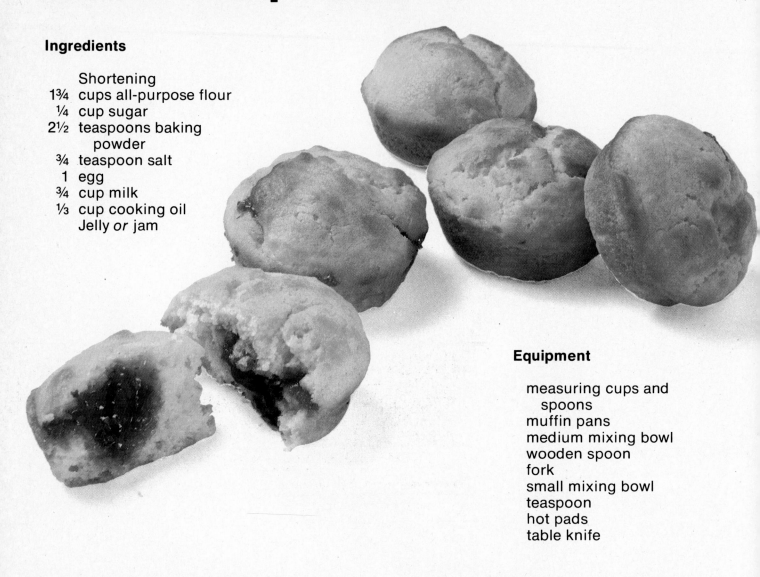

Equipment

measuring cups and spoons
muffin pans
medium mixing bowl
wooden spoon
fork
small mixing bowl
teaspoon
hot pads
table knife

1 With adult help, turn oven to 400°. Grease 12 muffin pans with some shortening. (Or put a paper bake cup into each muffin cup.)

2 Measure the flour, sugar, baking powder, and salt into the medium mixing bowl. Stir to mix with a wooden spoon.

3 Use a fork to beat the egg in the small mixing bowl. Add milk and oil. Beat with fork till well mixed.

4 Pour milk mixture over flour mixture. Stir with wooden spoon only till all flour is wet. Batter should be lumpy. Do not stir too much or muffins will be hard.

5 Spoon half the batter into muffin pans till each cup is about ⅓ full. Put a teaspoonful of jelly or jam on the batter in each cup. Fill muffin cups with remaining batter.

6 With adult help, put pan into oven. Bake till muffins are golden. This will take 20 to 25 minutes. Turn off oven.

7 With adult help, remove muffins from oven. Remove muffins from pan with a table knife. Cool 5 minutes.

Makes 12 muffins.

Corny Corn Bread

Ingredients

   Shortening
1 12-ounce can whole
    kernel corn with sweet
    peppers
1 cup yellow cornmeal
1 cup all-purpose flour
¼ cup sugar
1 tablespoon baking
    powder
1 teaspoon salt
2 eggs
1¼ cups milk
¼ cup cooking oil

Equipment

measuring cups and spoons
can opener
9x9x2-inch baking pan
sieve
medium mixing bowl
large mixing bowl
wooden spoon
small mixing bowl
fork
hot pads
table knife

1 Grease the 9x9x2-inch baking pan with some shortening. Put sieve over medium bowl. Empty corn into sieve and let it drain. Pour off liquid in bowl.

2 Measure cornmeal, flour, sugar, baking powder, and salt into large bowl. Stir with a wooden spoon till well mixed.

3 In small bowl beat eggs with a fork. Add drained corn, milk, and oil to bowl. Stir with fork till well mixed. Add to flour mixture; stir with a wooden spoon till mixed.

4 Pour mixture into the greased pan. Put pan into oven. With adult help, turn oven to 425°. Bake till corn bread is golden. This will take 35 to 40 minutes. Turn off the oven.

5 With adult help, remove pan from oven. Cut bread into squares with a table knife. Serve warm.

Makes 9 servings.

French Toast

Ingredients

4 slices bread
2 eggs
½ cup milk
¼ teaspoon salt
Dash ground cinnamon

2 tablespoons butter *or* margarine
Maple-flavored syrup *or* cinnamon sugar

Equipment

cooling rack
paper towel
measuring cups and spoons
small bowl
eggbeater
pie plate
6-inch skillet
pancake turner

1 Put bread on rack. Cover with paper towel and leave overnight to dry out slightly.

2 In bowl beat eggs with eggbeater till foamy. Add milk, salt, and cinnamon. Beat till well mixed. Pour into pie plate.

3 Put ¼ of the butter or margarine in skillet. Put skillet on burner. With adult help, turn burner to medium-low heat.

4 Dip one slice of bread into egg mixture, then turn it over to coat other side. Put bread into the skillet. Cook till bottom is golden brown. Lift toast with pancake turner to see if bottom is brown.

5 Turn bread with the pancake turner. Cook till other side is golden. Remove bread from pan with pancake turner.

6 Repeat steps 3, 4, and 5 till you use all the bread and egg mixture. Turn off burner. Serve with syrup or cinnamon sugar.

Makes 4 servings.

Pancakes

Ingredients

1 egg
1 cup milk
1 tablespoon cooking oil
1¼ cups all-purpose flour
2 tablespoons sugar

2 teaspoons baking powder
½ teaspoon salt
Cooking oil
Maple-flavored syrup *or* fresh fruit

Equipment

measuring cups and spoons
1-quart jar with lid
rubber scraper
paper towel
griddle
pancake turner

1 Break egg into jar. Stir with rubber scraper. Add milk and 1 tablespoon of oil. Screw lid on tightly. Shake to mix well.

2 Carefully measure flour, sugar, baking powder, and salt into the jar. Close lid tightly. Shake to mix well. Batter should have some lumps.

3 Use paper towel to rub a little cooking oil over the griddle. Put griddle on burner. With adult help, turn burner to medium heat.

4 Heat the griddle. Sprinkle a few drops of water on the griddle. If they jump, the griddle is hot enough to use. Measure ¼ cup batter for each pancake and pour onto hot griddle. Cook 3 or 4 at a time.

5 When bubbles cover surface of pancake and edges look dry, turn over with pancake turner. Cook till golden brown.

6 Remove pancakes with pancake turner. Repeat till you use all the batter. Put a little more oil on griddle if pancakes stick. Turn off burner. Serve with syrup or fruit.

Makes 7 or 8 pancakes.

Pick-a-Top Biscuits

Ingredients

1½ cups all-purpose flour
1½ teaspoons baking powder
¾ teaspoon salt
½ cup milk
¼ cup cooking oil

Pick a topper (choose one of the following):

2 tablespoons grated parmesan cheese
2 tablespoons sesame seed
2 tablespoons poppy seed
1 tablespoon sugar mixed with ¼ teaspoon ground cinnamon

Equipment

measuring cups and spoons
medium mixing bowl
spoon
small bowl
fork
waxed paper
ruler
table knife
pancake turner
baking sheet
hot pads

1 With adult help, turn oven to 450°. Measure flour, baking powder, and salt into the medium mixing bowl. Stir with a spoon to mix.

2 In a small bowl mix milk and oil. Pour all at once over flour mixture. Stir with a fork till well mixed.

3 Put dough on a sheet of waxed paper. Knead lightly 10 times or till smooth. Pat out with your hands to make a 6-inch square, as shown. Sprinkle your favorite topping over the dough. Press in lightly with your hands. (Or leave dough plain.)

4 Use a table knife to cut dough into 9 squares. Use a pancake turner to put each square on the baking sheet.

5 With adult help, use hot pads to put pan into hot oven. Bake till biscuits are golden. This will take 12 to 15 minutes. Turn off oven. With adult help, remove pan from oven. To serve, put biscuits on a plate with a pancake turner. Serve immediately.

Makes 9 biscuits.

Press down on the dough with your hands and shape it into a 6-inch square. Measure with a ruler to make sure it is the right size, then cut it into 9 squares.

No-Knead Yeast Rolls

Ingredients

  2   cups all-purpose flour
  1   package active dry yeast
1¼ cups milk
 ½ cup butter *or* margarine
 ¼ cup sugar
  1   teaspoon salt
  1   egg
1¼ cups all-purpose *or*
     whole wheat flour
     Shortening

Equipment

   measuring cups
     and spoons
   large mixer bowl
   wooden spoon
   1-quart saucepan
   thermometer
   electric stand mixer
   waxed paper
   muffin pans
   hot pads

Milk mixture should not be hotter than 115°. Check with a thermometer or ask adult to show you how to test a baby bottle.

1 In large mixer bowl mix the 2 cups flour and yeast with a wooden spoon.

2 Put milk, butter, sugar, and salt into saucepan. Put pan on burner. With adult help, turn burner to medium heat. Cook and stir till butter melts and mixture is warm (115°), as shown. Turn off burner.

3 Pour warm mixture over flour mixture. Add egg. With adult help, beat at low speed with mixer for 30 seconds. Beat at high speed 3 minutes. Remove bowl from mixer.

4 Gradually stir in the 1¼ cups all-purpose or whole wheat flour. Beat with wooden spoon till smooth.

5 Grease waxed paper with some shortening. Cover dough in bowl with the waxed paper. Put in a warm place to rise for 1 hour or till dough is twice as big.

6 Beat dough with a wooden spoon. Let rest 5 minutes. Grease 20 muffin pans with shortening.

7 Drop batter with a spoon into muffin pans, filling them about halfway. Cover with greased waxed paper and let rise 30 minutes or till twice as big. About 10 minutes before time is up, ask an adult to help you turn oven to 400°.

8 Remove waxed paper. With adult help, put pans into oven. Bake 12 to 15 minutes or till golden. Turn off oven. With adult help, remove rolls from oven. Serve warm.

Makes 20.

Something Different

Yeast Loaf: Pour batter into greased 9x5x3-inch loaf pan. Let rise. Bake in 375° oven 45 minutes. Cool before slicing.

Pumpkin-Nut Bread

Ingredients

Shortening
2 cups all-purpose flour
2 teaspoons baking powder
½ teaspoon salt
½ teaspoon pumpkin pie spice
¼ teaspoon baking soda

1 cup packed brown sugar
⅓ cup shortening
2 eggs
1 cup canned pumpkin
¼ cup milk
½ cup chopped walnuts (if you like)

Equipment

measuring cups and spoons
can opener
9x5x3-inch loaf pan
small mixing bowl
wooden spoon
medium mixing bowl
rubber scraper
hot pads
cooling rack

1 Grease bottom of loaf pan with shortening. With adult help, turn oven to 350°.

2 In small bowl use a wooden spoon to stir together flour, baking powder, salt, pumpkin pie spice, and soda.

3 In medium bowl use a wooden spoon to beat brown sugar and the ⅓ cup shortening, till mixed. Add one egg and beat well. Add the other egg and beat well. Stir in pumpkin and milk.

4 Stir in flour mixture just till smooth. Do not stir too much. Stir in nuts. Spread evenly in greased pan, scraping bowl with rubber scraper.

5 With adult help, put pan into oven. Bake for 1 hour. Turn off oven. With adult help, remove pan from oven and put on cooling rack. Cool for 10 minutes. Remove bread from pan and cool completely on rack.

Makes 1 loaf.

Apple-Nut Coffee Cake

Ingredients

Shortening
1 cup all-purpose flour
½ teaspoon baking powder
½ teaspoon baking soda
⅛ teaspoon salt
½ cup regular sugar
¼ cup shortening
1 egg
½ teaspoon vanilla
1 large apple
½ cup dairy sour cream
¼ cup nuts
¼ cup packed brown sugar
1 tablespoon butter
½ teaspoon ground cinnamon

To make Sunrise Juice: pour apricot nectar into a glass. Tilt glass and slowly add cranberry juice cocktail.

Equipment

measuring cups
and spoons
9x9x2-inch baking pan
mixing bowls
wooden spoon
vegetable peeler
sharp knife
cutting board
rubber scraper
plastic bag
rolling pin
hot pads

1 Grease pan with some shortening. In medium bowl stir together flour, baking powder, soda, and salt.

2 In large mixing bowl use a wooden spoon to beat together regular sugar and the ¼ cup shortening till fluffy. Beat in egg and vanilla till well mixed.

3 Peel apple with vegetable peeler. With adult help, remove core from apple and throw it away. Chop the apple.

4 Stir about *half* the flour mixture into the sugar mixture. Stir in sour cream. Stir in the rest of the flour mixture.

5 Stir in chopped apple. Spread evenly in greased pan, scraping bowl with rubber scraper.

6 Put nuts into plastic bag. Close bag and crush nuts with the rolling pin. Empty bag into small bowl. Use your hands to mix in brown sugar, butter, and cinnamon. Sprinkle over coffee cake. Put pan into oven.

7 With adult help, turn oven to 350°. Bake 25 to 30 minutes or till done. Turn off oven. With adult help, remove pan from oven. Cut into pieces and serve warm.

Makes 9 to 12 servings.

Anytime Treats

Here are lots of recipes for milk shakes and other drinks, cookies, desserts, and treats—all your favorite snack foods! Take them to school, to scout meetings, or to a party of your own. When your friends find out what a good cook you are, they will want to learn, too. These two cooks are working on Fruity Cutouts (the recipe is on page 81).

Strawberry Shakes

Ingredients

1 10-ounce package frozen
   strawberries, thawed
1 cup milk
1 pint strawberry ice cream
   or frozen yogurt
   (2 cups)

Equipment

measuring cup
blender
ice cream scoop *or* large
   spoon
3 tall glasses
long-handled spoons
straws

1 Put strawberries and their juice into blender container. With adult help, cover and blend till smooth. Add the milk. Cover and blend till smooth.

2 Scoop some of the ice cream or yogurt into each of 3 tall glasses. Put the rest of the ice cream or yogurt into the blender container. With adult help, cover and blend till smooth.

3 Pour mixture from blender over the ice cream or yogurt in glasses. Serve with long-handled spoons and straws. Top each with a whole strawberry, if you like.

Makes 3 servings.

Something Different

Chocolate Soda: Pour 2 tablespoons of *chocolate-flavored syrup* into a tall glass. Add a large spoonful of vanilla or chocolate *ice cream* and stir till mixed. Add enough *carbonated water* to fill the glass halfway. Stir gently to mix. Add 1 or 2 scoops of vanilla or chocolate ice cream, and finish filling the glass with carbonated water. Serve with a long-handled spoon and a straw. Makes 1 soda.

Apricot-Banana Shakes

Ingredients

- 1 cup orange juice, chilled
- ½ cup milk
- ¼ teaspoon vanilla
- 1 16-ounce can pitted apricot halves, chilled
- 1 banana
  Ground nutmeg

Equipment

measuring cups and spoons
can opener
blender
glasses

1 Measure the orange juice, milk, and vanilla into the blender container. Add apricots and their juice. Peel banana. Break banana into 4 pieces; add to blender container.

2 With adult help, cover the blender and blend till smooth. Pour into glasses; sprinkle with a little nutmeg.

Makes 4 servings.

Chocolate Shakes

Ingredients

- ¾ cup milk
- 3 tablespoons chocolate-flavored syrup
- 1 pint vanilla ice cream (2 cups)

Equipment

measuring cup and spoons
blender
ice cream scoop *or* large spoon
glasses

1 Pour milk into blender container. Add the chocolate syrup. With adult help, cover and blend till smooth.

2 Add *half* the ice cream; cover and blend till smooth. Add the rest of the ice cream; cover and blend just till smooth. Pour into glasses.

Makes 2 servings.

Something Different

Peanut-Cocoa Shakes: Follow recipe above *but* add 2 tablespoons peanut butter when you add the chocolate syrup.

Banana-Cocoa Shakes: Follow recipe above *but* add half a banana each time you add ice cream.

Hot Cocoa

Ingredients

⅓ cup sugar
⅓ cup unsweetened cocoa
    powder
Dash salt
½ cup water
3½ cups milk
½ teaspoon vanilla

Equipment

measuring cups and spoons
1½-quart saucepan
wooden spoon
eggbeater
ladle
4 mugs

1 In pan mix sugar, cocoa, and salt. Slowly stir in water. Put pan on burner. With adult help, turn burner to medium heat. Cook and stir till mixture boils. Boil 1 minute, stirring all the time.

2 Add milk, 1 cup at a time, stirring as you do. Heat and stir till mixture just starts to bubble around the edge of pan. Turn off burner. With adult help, move pan off burner. Stir in vanilla.

3 Use eggbeater to beat till foamy. Be careful not to splatter. Ladle into mugs. Top with marshmallows or marshmallow creme, if you like.

Makes 4 servings.

Easy Cocoa Mix

Ingredients:

1 9.6-ounce package
    (4 cups) nonfat dry
    milk powder
1 8-ounce can (1½ cups)
    presweetened cocoa
    powder
1 3-ounce jar (¾ cup)
    non-dairy creamer

Equipment

large mixing bowl
wooden spoon
covered container

1 In large mixing bowl stir all ingredients together. Store in covered container.

2 To serve, put ⅓ cup mix in a mug. With adult help, stir in ⅔ cup *boiling water*. This makes enough mix for 19 servings.

Spicy Cider

Ingredients

4 cups apple cider *or* juice
¼ cup red cinnamon
candies

Equipment

measuring cups
2-quart saucepan
wooden spoon
cups *or* mugs

1 Pour cider or juice into saucepan. Add cinnamon candies. Put pan on burner. With adult help, turn burner to medium heat. Heat and stir till candies melt and cider is hot. Turn off burner.

2 With adult help, pour spicy cider into cups or mugs. Serve each with a cinnamon stick, if you like.

Makes 4 to 6 servings.

Orange Cider

Ingredients

1 cup apple cider *or* juice
1½ teaspoons orange-
flavored breakfast
drink powder
Dash ground nutmeg
Dash ground cinnamon

Equipment

measuring cup and
spoons
1-quart saucepan
mug
spoon

1 Pour cider into pan. Put on burner. With adult help, turn burner to high heat. When cider is hot, turn off burner. Pour into mug.

2 Add drink powder, nutmeg, and cinnamon. Stir with a spoon or candy sticks.

Makes 1 serving.

Frozen Chocolate Bananas

Ingredients

¼ cup chopped peanuts
½ cup milk chocolate
    pieces *or* semisweet
    chocolate pieces
1 large banana

Equipment

measuring cups
shallow bowl
waxed paper
plate
small skillet
wooden spoon
cutting board
table knife
2 wooden sticks
plastic wrap *or* foil

1 Put chopped peanuts into shallow bowl.
Put a piece of waxed paper on a plate.

2 Put chocolate pieces into skillet. Put skillet
on burner. With adult help, turn burner to
low heat. Stir all the time with wooden
spoon till chocolate melts. Turn off burner.
Remove skillet from heat.

3 Peel banana. Throw away the peel.
On cutting board, cut banana in
half with table knife. Push a
wooden stick into cut end of
each banana half. Use table
knife to spread chocolate
on all sides of banana
halves. Immediately roll
in peanuts to coat.

4 Put bananas on waxed
paper-lined plate. Freeze
till hard. If you want to save
for another day, wrap frozen
bananas in plastic wrap or foil.

Makes 2 servings.

Something Different

Coconut-Chocolate Bananas: Follow
recipe above, *but* roll bananas in ¼ cup
flaked coconut instead of the peanuts.

Creamy Punch

Ingredients

1 ½-gallon carton vanilla
   ice cream
4 cups orange juice
½ cup lemon juice

2 28-ounce bottles
   lemon-lime
   carbonated beverage,
   chilled

Equipment

measuring cups
large spoon
punch bowl and cups
ladle

1 Spoon the ice cream into the punch bowl. Add the orange juice and the lemon juice. Stir with the large spoon.

2 Slowly add the lemon-lime beverage. Stir gently. Punch will be very foamy. Ladle into punch cups.

Makes about 25 servings.

Berry Punch

Ingredients

1 3-ounce package
   strawberry- *or*
   raspberry-flavored
   gelatin
½ cup sugar
2½ cups water
2 cups cold water

1 10-ounce package frozen
   strawberries *or*
   raspberries
1 6-ounce can frozen
   lemonade concentrate
1 28-ounce bottle
   lemon-lime
   carbonated beverage,
   chilled
   Ice cubes

Equipment

measuring cups
can opener
large mixing bowl
wooden spoon
teakettle
punch bowl and cups
ladle

1 In large bowl combine gelatin and sugar. Put about 2½ cups of water into teakettle. Put kettle on burner. With adult help, turn burner to high heat. When water boils, turn off burner. With adult help, measure 2 cups of boiling water. Pour into bowl with gelatin mixture. Stir till all gelatin dissolves.

2 Stir in the 2 cups cold water, the frozen berries, and the lemonade concentrate. Stir till berries and lemonade are thawed. Chill mixture till serving time.

3 With adult help, pour mixture into punch bowl. Add the lemon-lime beverage and ice. Ladle into punch cups.

Makes about 20 servings.

Frozen Fruit Pops

You can make these tasty treats by yourself, but discuss it with an adult first—

Ingredients

3 cups strawberries
1 cup water
⅔ cup sugar
1 envelope unsweetened strawberry- *or* cherry-flavored soft drink mix

Equipment

measuring cups
mixing bowl
potato masher *or* fork
wooden spoon
3-ounce waxed paper drink cups *or* frozen pop molds
muffin pan
foil
table knife
wooden sticks

1 Wash strawberries under cold water. Pull off stems and leaves with your fingers. Put strawberries into bowl. Mash with potato masher or fork till almost smooth.

2 Stir in water, sugar, and soft drink mix till mixed. Pour mixture into 12 to 16 drink cups or pop molds till almost full. Use a muffin pan to hold cups steady, if you need to.

3 Cover each cup with foil. Make a little hole in foil with knife. Push a stick into cup through hole. Freeze 4 to 6 hours or till firm. To serve, tear off paper or remove from the molds.

Makes 12 to 16 pops.

Something Different

Banana-Fruit Pops: Follow the recipe above, *but* use 4 large bananas instead of the strawberries. Peel the bananas and mash them in the bowl.

Fruity Cutouts

Ingredients

½ cup sugar
4 envelopes unflavored
   gelatin
   Dash salt
2½ cups pineapple juice,
   apple juice, orange
   juice, grape juice, *or*
   fruit-flavored drink

Equipment

measuring cups
mixing bowl
rubber scraper
1-quart saucepan
13x9x2-inch pan
small cookie cutters
pancake turner

1 In mixing bowl stir sugar, gelatin, and salt with rubber scraper till well mixed.

2 Put fruit juice into 1-quart saucepan. Put pan on burner. With adult help, turn burner to high heat. Cook till juice boils. Turn off burner.

3 With adult help, pour boiling fruit juice over sugar mixture. Stir with a rubber scraper till all gelatin is dissolved. Pour into 13x9x2-inch pan. Put into refrigerator and chill till firm.

4 Use small cookie cutters to cut shapes from the gelatin in the pan. Remove shapes from pan with pancake turner. Eat with your fingers.

Something Different

When you are through cutting out shapes, you will have some scraps left over. Put the scraps back into the saucepan. Put pan on burner. With adult help, turn burner to low heat. Cook and stir till scraps melt. Turn off burner. Pour melted mixture into a smaller pan and chill till firm, then use a table knife to cut into squares or diamonds.

Be sure to mix hot fruit juice and gelatin well, so your cutouts won't have any lumps in them.

Brownies

Ingredients

- Shortening
- ¾ cup butter *or* margarine
- 2 squares (2 ounces) unsweetened chocolate
- 1⅓ cups sugar
- 3 eggs
- 1 cup all-purpose flour
- 1 teaspoon baking powder
- ½ teaspoon salt

Equipment

measuring cups and spoons
13x9x2-inch baking pan
2-quart saucepan
wooden spoon
small mixing bowl

rubber scraper
hot pads
cooling rack
knife
pancake turner

1 With adult help, turn oven to 350°. Grease the baking pan with some shortening.

2 Put butter and chocolate into saucepan. Put on burner. With adult help, turn burner to low heat. Heat till butter and chocolate melt, stirring once or twice. Turn off burner and remove pan.

3 Stir sugar into chocolate mixture. Stir in the 3 eggs, 1 egg at a time, till well mixed.

4 In a small bowl mix flour, baking powder, and salt. Stir into chocolate mixture. Scrape into the greased pan and spread out with rubber scraper. With adult help, put pan into oven. Bake for 25 to 30 minutes. Turn off oven.

5 With adult help, remove pan from oven. Cool pan on rack. When cool, sprinkle with powdered sugar, if you like. Cut into bars. Use pancake turner to remove.

Makes 24 to 36 brownies.

Snickerdoodles

Ingredients

¾ cup sugar
½ cup butter *or* margarine
1 egg
½ teaspoon vanilla
1½ cups all-purpose flour
¼ teaspoon salt
¼ teaspoon baking soda
¼ teaspoon cream of tartar
2 tablespoons sugar
2 teaspoons ground
   cinnamon
Shortening

Equipment

measuring cups and spoons
large mixing bowl
wooden spoon
small mixing bowl
spoon

cookie sheets
ruler
hot pads
pancake turner
cooling rack

1 In large mixing bowl cream the ¾ cup sugar and the butter or margarine with a wooden spoon. Beat in the egg and vanilla.

2 In small bowl stir together flour, salt, baking soda, and cream of tartar. Stir into butter mixture with wooden spoon till well mixed.

3 In the same small bowl combine the 2 tablespoons sugar and the cinnamon.

4 With adult help, turn oven to 375°. Grease 1 or 2 cookie sheets with some shortening.

5 Shape dough into 1-inch balls; roll each in the sugar-cinnamon mixture. Put balls 2 inches apart on greased cookie sheet. With adult help, put pan into oven. Bake 8 to 10 minutes. With adult help, remove from oven. Use pancake turner to put cookies on rack. Turn off oven.

Makes about 36.

Peanut Butter Cookies

Ingredients

- 1 cup shortening
- 1 cup peanut butter
- 1 cup regular sugar
- 1 cup packed brown sugar
- 2 eggs
- 1 teaspoon vanilla
- 2¼ cups all-purpose flour
- 2 teaspoons baking soda
- ¼ teaspoon salt

Equipment

- measuring cups and spoons
- large mixing bowl
- wooden spoon
- medium mixing bowl
- spoon
- cookie sheets
- hot pads
- pancake turner
- cooling rack

1 In large bowl mix shortening and peanut butter with wooden spoon. Add both kinds of sugar. Stir till mixed. Stir in eggs and vanilla till mixed.

2 In medium bowl stir together flour, soda, and salt. Stir into sugar mixture till well mixed. Use your hands to mix the dough, if you need to. With adult help, turn oven to 350°.

3 Form dough into balls and ropes. Put on ungreased cookie sheets. Push together and flatten with your hands to make people and other shapes.

4 With adult help, put cookie sheet into oven. Bake for 10 to 12 minutes. With adult help, remove from oven. Let cool on pan 1 minute. Use pancake turner to put cookies on rack to finish cooling. Repeat steps 3 and 4 with rest of dough. Turn off oven.

Makes about 36 large cookies.

Oatmeal Cookies

Ingredients

    1 cup all-purpose flour
    ½ cup regular sugar
    ½ cup packed brown sugar
    ½ teaspoon salt
    ½ teaspoon baking soda
    ½ cup shortening
    1 egg
    2 tablespoons milk
    ½ teaspoon vanilla
 1½ cups quick-cooking
       rolled oats
    1 cup semisweet chocolate
       pieces *or* raisins
       Shortening

Equipment

measuring cups and spoons
large mixing bowl
wooden spoon
cookie sheets
teaspoons
hot pads
pancake turner
cooling rack

1 In large mixing bowl stir together the flour, both kinds of sugar, salt, and soda. Add the ½ cup shortening, egg, milk, and vanilla. Stir with wooden spoon till well mixed, or mix with your hands. Mix in the oats and the chocolate pieces or raisins.

2 With adult help, turn oven to 350°. Grease 1 or 2 cookie sheets with some shortening.

3 Drop dough from a teaspoon to make small mounds about 2 inches apart on greased cookie sheet. Push dough off one spoon with another spoon.

4 With adult help, put cookie sheet into oven. Bake for 12 minutes. With adult help, remove from oven. Use pancake turner to lift cookies onto cooling rack. Repeat steps 3 and 4 with rest of dough. Turn off oven.

Makes about 50.

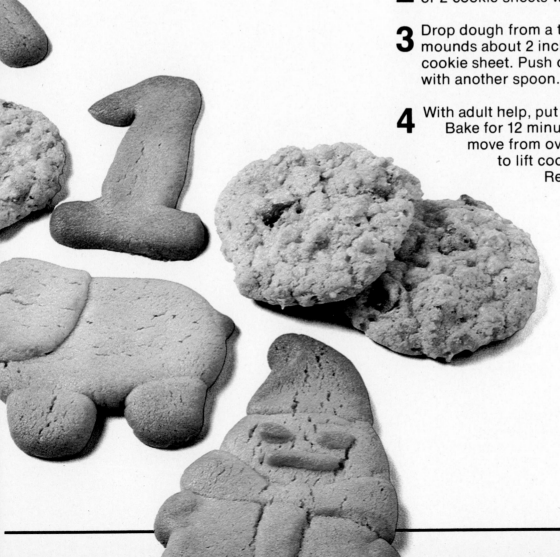

Yellow Cake

Ingredients

Shortening
All-purpose flour
⅓ cup shortening
1½ cups all-purpose flour
¾ cup sugar
2½ teaspoons baking powder
½ teaspoon salt
¾ cup milk
1 egg
1½ teaspoons vanilla

Equipment

measuring cups and spoons
9x9x2-inch square *or*
  9x1½-inch round baking pan
small mixer bowl
electric mixer
rubber scraper
hot pads
wooden pick
cooling rack

1 Grease pan with about 1 tablespoon shortening. Add 1 tablespoon flour and shake till coated; dump out extra flour. With adult help, turn oven to 375°.

2 Put ⅓ cup shortening into bowl. Add 1½ cups flour, sugar, baking powder, and salt. Add *half* of milk, the egg, and vanilla.

3 With adult help, use electric mixer to beat at low speed till mixed. Beat at medium speed 2 minutes. Scrape sides of bowl with rubber scraper. Add rest of milk. Beat at low speed till mixed. Beat at medium speed 2 minutes. Scrape batter into pan.

4 With adult help, put pan into oven. Bake for 30 minutes. Check to see if cake is done by pushing a wooden pick into center. If you pull pick out without any cake sticking, the cake is done. Turn off oven.

5 With adult help, remove cake from oven. Cool on rack. Remove cake from pan, if you like. Frost cooled cake with Butter Frosting (see recipe on next page), if you like. Decorate with candies.

Butter Frosting

Ingredients

3 tablespoons butter *or* margarine, softened
2⅓ cups sifted powdered sugar
Milk
¾ teaspoon vanilla

Equipment

measuring cups and spoons
sifter
small mixer bowl
electric mixer
rubber scraper

1 Put butter or margarine into mixer bowl. With adult help, beat with electric mixer at low speed till fluffy. Scrape bowl with rubber scraper. Add about *half* the sugar, while beating at low speed.

2 Beat in *1 tablespoon* milk and the vanilla at low speed. Slowly add the rest of the powdered sugar, beating constantly. Beat in more milk if you need it to make frosting easy to spread. Spread over a cooled cake.

3 This recipe makes enough frosting for a one-layer cake. If you need to frost 2 layers, ask an adult to help you double the amounts of ingredients.

Something Different

Chocolate Butter Frosting: Prepare frosting as directed in the recipe above, *but*, with adult help, melt 1 square (1 ounce) unsweetened chocolate. Cool and add to frosting with the vanilla.

Filled Cupcakes

Ingredients

1 3-ounce package cream
   cheese, softened
¼ cup sugar
2 tablespoons chopped
   nuts
½ teaspoon vanilla
⅔ cup all-purpose flour
¼ cup unsweetened cocoa
   powder

1 teaspoon baking powder
½ cup sugar
¼ cup butter *or* margarine,
   softened
1 egg
½ teaspoon vanilla
½ cup milk

Equipment

measuring cups and spoons
12 paper bake cups
muffin pans
2 small mixing bowls
spoon
wooden spoon
medium mixing bowl
hot pads
cooling rack

1 With adult help, turn oven to 375°. Put 12 paper bake cups into muffin pans. In a small bowl use the spoon to stir the cream cheese, the ¼ cup sugar, nuts, and ½ teaspoon vanilla till mixed.

2 In small bowl mix flour, cocoa, and baking powder with wooden spoon. In medium bowl cream the ½ cup sugar and butter with wooden spoon till fluffy. Stir in egg and ½ teaspoon vanilla till mixed.

3 Stir about *half* the flour mixture into the butter mixture. Slowly stir in milk till smooth. Stir in the rest of the flour mixture till smooth.

4 Spoon about 1 tablespoon batter into each bake cup. Add about 1 teaspoon of nut mixture to each. Finish filling with batter.

5 With adult help, put pan into oven. Bake 20 minutes. Turn off oven. With adult help, remove pan from oven and cupcakes from pan. Cool on rack.

Makes 12 cupcakes.

Chocolate-Nut Balls

Make these treats by yourself once you've read the recipe with an adult—

Ingredients

- 66 vanilla wafers
- 1 cup walnuts
- 1 cup sifted powdered sugar
- ¼ cup unsweetened cocoa powder
- ⅓ cup orange juice
- 3 tablespoons honey
- ½ cup sifted powdered sugar

Equipment

measuring cups and spoons
sifter
heavy plastic bag
rolling pin
mixing bowls
wooden spoon

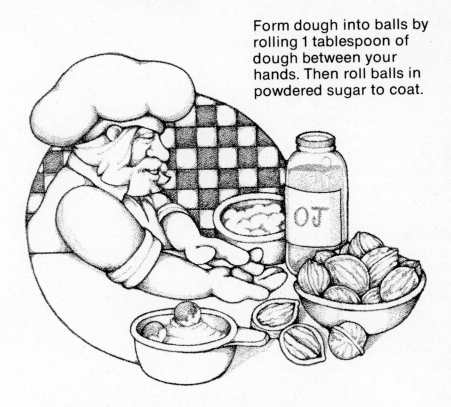

Form dough into balls by rolling 1 tablespoon of dough between your hands. Then roll balls in powdered sugar to coat.

1 Put *half* the vanilla wafers into a heavy plastic bag; push air out and close tightly. Use a rolling pin to crush wafers into tiny crumbs. Pour into large bowl. Repeat with remaining wafers. You should have a little less than 3 cups of crumbs.

2 Put the walnuts into the plastic bag and close tightly. Use rolling pin to crush the walnuts into tiny crumbs. Add to the crumbs in bowl.

3 Use a wooden spoon to stir in the 1 cup powdered sugar and the cocoa powder. Add the orange juice and honey. Stir till well mixed. Add 1 or 2 tablespoons more orange juice, if needed.

4 Use 1 tablespoon mixture for each cookie. Shape into balls with your hands, as shown. Put the ½ cup powdered sugar into small bowl. Roll balls in powdered sugar to coat, shaking off any extra sugar. Store in airtight container.

Makes about 40.

Peanut Butter Granola

Ingredients

2 cups rolled oats
1 cup wheat germ
½ cup sesame seed
½ cup coconut
⅔ cup peanut butter
½ cup honey
2 tablespoons cooking oil
1 teaspoon vanilla
½ teaspoon salt

Equipment

measuring cups and
   spoons
13x9x2-inch baking pan
rubber scraper
small mixing bowl
hot pads
pancake turner
covered container

Break up the granola with a pancake turner. Lift the mixture with the turner and let it drop back into the pan.

1 Measure the oats, wheat germ, sesame seed, and coconut into the baking pan. Stir with rubber scraper to mix.

2 In the small bowl use the rubber scraper to stir together the peanut butter, honey, cooking oil, vanilla, and salt. Pour over the oat mixture. Stir with rubber scraper till all is coated.

3 Put pan into oven. With adult help, turn oven to 300°. Bake for 45 minutes. Turn off the oven.

4 With adult help, use hot pads to remove pan from oven. Stir mixture with a pancake turner to break up, as shown. Let granola cool. Store in covered container. Eat for a snack or as a breakfast cereal.

Makes about 6 cups.

Something Different

Make granola into your own special creation with a few extra ingredients. To the rolled oat mixture, you can add ½ cup shelled sunflower seeds, chopped peanuts, chopped almonds, or other chopped nuts instead of the sesame seed.

When granola has baked and cooled, you can add about ½ cup dried fruit, cut into small pieces. Try fruits such as dried apricots, dried apples, prunes, raisins, and mixed dried fruits.

Hot Fudge Pudding Cake

Ingredients

1 cup all-purpose flour
2 tablespoons unsweetened cocoa powder
2 teaspoons baking powder
¼ teaspoon salt
½ cup milk
½ cup honey

2 tablespoons cooking oil
1 teaspoon vanilla
¾ cup packed brown sugar
¼ cup unsweetened cocoa powder
1¾ cups hot water

Equipment

measuring cups and spoons
9x9x2-inch baking pan
fork
small bowl
hot pads
cooling rack
large spoon

1 Measure the flour, the 2 tablespoons cocoa powder, the baking powder, and salt into the baking pan. Stir with fork to mix well.

2 Add the milk, honey, cooking oil, and vanilla. Stir with the fork till smooth. Spread evenly in the pan.

3 Use your fingers to mix the brown sugar and the ¼ cup cocoa in a small bowl. Sprinkle over the batter. Pour the hot water over sugar and cocoa, as shown. Do not stir.

4 With adult help, put pan in oven. Turn oven to 350°. Bake for 40 minutes. Mixture will form a cake and a sauce in the pan. Turn off the oven.

5 With adult help, remove pan from oven and put on cooling rack. Let stand for 15 minutes to cool slightly.

6 To serve, use a large spoon to put cake and sauce into dessert dishes. Serve with ice cream, if you like.

Makes 9 servings.

Measure 1¾ cups hot water from the faucet. Pour over the mixture in the baking pan.

Creamy Lemon Pie

Ingredients

3 lemons
1 egg
1 14-ounce can *sweetened condensed* milk
1 4½-ounce carton frozen whipped dessert topping, thawed
1 9-inch graham cracker crust

Equipment

measuring cup and spoons
can opener
grater
waxed paper
sharp knife
cutting board
juicer
mixing bowl
fork
rubber scraper
plastic wrap

1 With adult help, put grater over waxed paper and grate peel from 1 lemon. Measure 1 teaspoon of peel to use in this recipe. Cut all the lemons in half and squeeze with juicer. Measure ½ cup of lemon juice to use in this recipe.

2 Break egg into bowl. Beat with a fork till white and yolk are mixed.

3 Pour the sweetened condensed milk into bowl with egg. Add the grated lemon peel and lemon juice. Stir with rubber scraper till mixture starts to thicken. Carefully fold in the dessert topping.

4 Pour filling into graham cracker crust. Cover with plastic wrap. Put into refrigerator for several hours or till firm. *Or* put into the freezer till pie is frozen. If you like, top pie with a curled slice of lemon.

On Top On Top

If it's okay with your adult helper, you can make this dessert by yourself—

Ingredients

1 8½-ounce package chocolate wafers (40)
1 9-ounce carton frozen whipped dessert topping, thawed
2 tablespoons small colored candies

Equipment

measuring spoons
8x8x2-inch square pan *or* dish
rubber scraper
plastic wrap *or* foil

1 Arrange one layer of 10 chocolate wafers in the square pan or dish. Break up some of the cookies to fit into the holes.

2 Use a rubber scraper to spread about ¼ of the thawed dessert topping over the cookies. Cover them so you can't see the cookies.

3 Repeat steps 1 and 2 till all the cookies and the dessert topping are used. The top layer should be dessert topping. Sprinkle the top with the candies.

4 Cover the pan or dish with plastic wrap or foil. Chill in refrigerator for at least 6 hours so cookies get soft.

Makes 8 servings.

Popcorn

Ingredients

1 tablespoon cooking oil
3 tablespoons unpopped
   popcorn
   Salt

Equipment

measuring spoons
heavy 2-quart saucepan *or*
   skillet with lid
large bowl

1 Pour cooking oil into heavy 2-quart saucepan or skillet. Add 2 or 3 kernels of the unpopped popcorn.

2 Put pan on the burner. With adult help, turn burner to medium-high heat. Put lid on pan and cook till you hear the corn pop.

3 Remove lid and add the rest of the popcorn. Put lid on pan and continue cooking, shaking the pan gently. When popping slows down, turn off the burner. Continue shaking pan till corn stops popping.

4 With adult help, pour popped corn into large bowl. Sprinkle with some salt.

Makes about 4 cups.

Something Different

Buttered Popcorn:

Fix popcorn, following recipe above. Put about 1 tablespoon *butter or margarine* into the same pan you used to cook the popcorn. Put on burner. With adult help, turn burner to low heat and heat till butter melts. Turn off burner. Pour over the salted popcorn. Mix with your hands.